WOMAN AT THE ALTAR

WOMAN AT THE ALTAR

The Ordination of Women in the Roman Catholic Church

LAVINIA BYRNE

Through the intricate metres of their slow advancement,
God, through his daughters here, is taking aim.
Thomas Blackburn, 'Luna',
Collected Poems (Hutchinson, 1975)

MOWBRAY

Mowbray
A Cassell imprint
Wellington House
125 Strand
London
WC2R 0BB

First published 1994. Reprinted 1998.

British Library Cataloguing-in-Publication Data
A catalogue entry for this book is available from the British Library.

ISBN 0-264-67335-2

Typeset by Litho Link Ltd, Welshpool, Powys, UK
Printed and bound in Great Britain by Mackays of Chatham PLC, Chatham, Kent

Contents

FOR

Angela Tilby

Introduction

This book is offered as a thanksgiving to all in our Churches who, over the past century, have sought to bring women and our ministry in God's service into the light. It seeks to explore the happiness and interest of those who rejoice in this development while not forgetting the suspicion and anxiety of those who question its legitimacy. A woman who comes to the altar as priest is a woman who moves from comparative invisibility to a place where the glory of Christ is recognized in her. This corresponds to a shift in all our Churches as new pastoral, social and other demands bring women from the obscurity of one limited set of roles into the public arena. Here something new is required of all men and women. About the inner life and outside calls on our time, about public service and private responsibilities. This is an exciting time because we are in a position to make theological sense of these conflicting demands. Uniquely, Christianity has always promised a message that would be ever old and ever new. Now is the time to offer a way forward which will neither polarize the attitudes of people who disagree with each other about what the proper role and dignity of the Christian woman should be, nor dismiss and abandon the Christian tradition by declaring it redundant. Whether we like it or not, much of the Church's teaching does not speak authoritatively to the experience of women who choose – whether under God's calling, or in complete ignorance of it – to move from the private sphere of home life and family to the public sphere of work in and for the world. It appears to have even less to offer to those who struggle with and are judged by the demands of both. This is why it is essential for further work to be done to bring fresh thinking to bear upon these questions.

For three years I have had the privilege of working with women and men who are doing this fresh thinking. They are well aware that the debate about the ordination of women comes at the end of a long set of questions. These are about the access of women to public life and to a public role in society. They are about the relationships between women and men in a changing world. They are about the nature of human community and morality and leadership. How can they best be answered? I believe that education and advocacy are no longer enough. The root question about priesthood and women now presses for attention and demands a theological solution.

When I wrote *Women before God* in 1988, I was concerned about ordination as an academic and pastoral question. Although I wrote there about different images of priesthood and enjoyed exploring their theological significance, I did not really see them as part of my world. In this book I draw deliberately on my experience as Associate Secretary for the Community of Women and Men in the Church at the Council of Churches for Britain and Ireland. For now I have met and worked with ordained women in many of our Churches. I now know women with vocations to the priesthood in the Catholic tradition. I also write quite deliberately as a Roman Catholic woman and a religious sister. This is because of a desire to chronicle what is happening in my own Church, as Roman Catholic women begin to identify vocations to the priesthood as the substance of God's call to them. How can this be? How can God be asking one thing of certain women in the Church when the Church itself formally teaches that only men may be ordained? How indeed. This is one of the many questions which this book attempts to answer, by tracing what it means to be a Roman Catholic woman in an age of change. An age of change about which the Church is neither neutral nor uncaring. An age of change which is calling forth from the Roman Catholic Church a new understanding of what it is to be a woman and to be made in the image and likeness of God.

I believe that it is not incidental that I am a member of a

Roman Catholic religious order. After all, the sisters have had
to do some of the most adventurous of the exploratory
thinking about the proper role and dignity of women in the
Church. For centuries we have carried most of the written
and unwritten scripts about what God calls or may call
women to do. I believe that it is not incidental either that
Mary Ward, the Englishwoman who founded my own
religious congregation in the early seventeenth century, did
so against the odds. She was condemned as a heretic and
schismatic because she wanted her sisters to be mobile, rather
than enclosed; to be apostolic in their spirituality, rather than
monastic; and to be governed by women, rather than by men.
And all this when cloistered life was the only known option.
One of her enemies wrote of her sisters, 'They labour for the
conversion of England like priests'. Nowadays we might be
happier with the words 'evangelism in England'. But the
point is that the earliest pioneers of alternative roles for
women in our Churches were opposed because they appeared
to be espousing priesthood. This is why Mary Ward was
deemed to be out of order. No surprise then that her memory
was deliberately written out of the Catholic memory and
imagination for over two hundred years. Now she is revered
as an incomparable woman – Pius XII's words, not my own
– but remains uncanonized.

Mary Ward is one of many women who founded apostolic
religious communities. In all our Churches we now have, as
an integral part of our tradition, many examples of women
who are called and sent by Christ into the world to serve as
preachers, teachers and missionaries. Catholicism has always
insisted that the ministry of the word and sacrament must not
be separated; so that nowadays, as women in general and
nuns in particular are called increasingly to exercise a
ministry of the word, the Catholic Church has a formidable
task ahead of it. For it is at least arguable that, by not
ordaining women, the Church is persisting in a separation of
teaching and sacramental authority which is both artificial
and false to the deepest instincts of Catholicism.

The early seventeenth century was characterized by
revolution and change. It provided a fiery crucible in which
Mary Ward and her first sisters could forge out a new role for

women. The circumstances of the late twentieth century are not entirely dissimilar. For that reason, in the first half of this book, I look at what the Church teaches about women and how this has influenced the self-understanding as well as the aspirations of present-day Roman Catholic women. Then I examine what feminism has contributed to the debate. What is it and how does it work? Only then can I ask what it is to make Christian community in an age of equal and shared partnership; how we are to search for moral norms which meet the needs of all; and how leadership is to be exercised to work authentically and faithfully for the whole Christian community.

God is calling women to priesthood. What does this mean? In the two final chapters of this book I draw certain conclusions about the work of women and the ordained ministry. But what is the understanding of priesthood which I seek to bring to this discussion? Firstly, I notice that different people have different associations with the word priest. Some of these may be because of their Church's tradition, some because of their personal experience. Whatever the formal teaching of our own Church about the nature of the ordained ministry, we will each bring a different personal understanding which has been coloured by our experience. At the same time I notice that it is hardly surprising that the word itself has carried various meanings for Christians down the centuries because its very origins identify it with a variety of sources.

So, what does it mean to be a priest? What can we learn when we look at these origins? The English word priest is derived from *presbyter* which carries a very simple meaning. It means old person. Presbyters were officers in the early Church who came to represent the authority of the *episkopoi* or overseers. If that were the only meaning, life would be simple. We might find that individuals were excluded from the priesthood on the grounds of age, but that would be all – rather than, say, men, or women. Our problem is that the word priest is also a translation of the Greek word *hiereus* (with its Latin translation *sacerdos*). Now this is a word which was used in pre-Christian Hellenistic religion for one who offers sacrifice to a god. It is also used in this sense, of sacrificing priest, of the High Priests of first-century Judaism (and earlier) who offered sacrifices in the Temple in Jerusalem.

So we have three cultural strands at work here: Greek, Jewish and early Christian. More than that, there is the overlay of two additional sets of meaning, one about oversight and one about sacrifice. Small wonder, then, that there are different meanings and emphases in present-day Christianity. Any attempt at analysis risks over-simplification therefore, as there are blurred lines and a variety of opinions. But, in general, it would be true to say that traditionally the word priesthood does not usually designate Protestant ministries. These stress the New Testament's emphasis on Christ as the only mediating priest who offers sacrifice to the Father for the sins of the people. This understanding of the work of Christ is set out most clearly in the Letter to the Hebrews. The theology of Hebrews suggests that Christ's sacrifice has wiped out the need for human sacrifices; and has, in particular, superseded the sacrifices of the Jerusalem Temple (which, at the time the Letter to the Hebrews was written, may well have just been destroyed). Protestant ministries of word and sacrament assume that the eucharistic celebrant (who may or may not be ordained) recalls the Passion of Jesus by re-telling the story; not by actions which make it re-effective. There is a representative ingredient here but the representative nature of ministry in Protestantism would be seen in general pastoral terms. The minister would most likely be understood as going out to other people as Jesus did, rather than in specifically sacrificial terms as one who officiates in the place of Christ. In fact it is worth remembering that this sacrificial understanding is genuinely distasteful to the Protestant imagination. The sacrifice of Christ on the cross is a perfect sacrifice, never to be repeated; the notion of a sacrificing priesthood is an aberration. Probably this is why the Churches of the Reform have found it easier to admit women to the ranks of the ordained. After all, traditionally women bring life into being; they do not destroy it. Or so we thought.

Now the developed Catholic emphasis is different. The early Church Fathers speak of the *presbyteroi* acting *in persona Christi*, in the person of Christ. This suggests a line of interpretation which sees the priesthood as representative of

Christ at the Last Supper and on the cross. Indeed a priest, in the Catholic tradition, has come to represent the *authority* of Christ as Lord of the Church, as prophet, priest and king, which means the power to exercise judgement over sin as well as to bring life into being. Add the ingredient of celibacy and the Church itself becomes the spouse of the priest; she over whom he is to exercise this authority.

This means that, in Catholicism, the representative nature of priesthood is tied into a hierarchical system of church leadership. Just as the bishop represents the authority and the sending power of God, so the priest represents the Christ figure – the one who is sent. This is a dynamic pattern which gives great energy and authority to those who send and those who are sent. Priesthood and leadership belong inseparably together.

In Anglicanism in particular there is an incarnational focus which is especially important here. The priest is not simply sent in some generic sense. Rather he or she is sent to somewhere, a named place. Hence the moving account given by Lord Runcie in the House of Lords on Tuesday 2 November 1993 when he spoke in favour of the Priests (Ordination of Women) Measure.

What is the essence of priesthood? It is the vocation of representing God to the human community and the human community to God. In our English tradition there is a link between the doctrine of the incarnation (God in human form) and the parish priest's commitment to a particular place and a particular community. The parson is a special person ordained to pray and celebrate the eucharist on behalf of all his parishioners, churchgoers or not. So the priest is there for everyone and represents the God who is there for everyone.

In days when exclusively male leadership has been abandoned in other walks of life, it seems undeniable that this representative role of the priest may actually be weakened by a solely male priesthood. The admission of women would be an enlargement and opening up of priesthood rather than its overturning. When men are selected for priesthood we look for certain qualities. We

look first for faith; and with it faithfulness, stickability and
the capacity to go on when the going gets tough. We look
for evidence of a life of prayer because prayer is required of
a priest, both to sustain the loneliness of the job and as a
sign of the way he is pointing others. We look for
commitment to people, both to challenge and to console
the strong and the weak, the gifted and the deprived. We
look for a willingness to live sacrificially: to choose the less
attractive job; to make do with a not very appealing
income; and to work long hours without obvious reward.
We look for leaders who can inspire without domineering,
whose model is that of the Good Shepherd rather than the
successful graduate of the management training school.

I believe there are many women who possess these
priestly qualities and whose ability to bring men and
women to God is tempered by the kind of tough gentleness
which nourishes families and challenges the overbearing.
Neither authoritarian nor submissive, these women are
bringing new life and integrity to the communities in which
they work. In my travels to other parts of the world, where
women are ordained as priests; I have seen this for myself.
In their ministry in partnership with men, they are
enabling those men to discover new gifts within
themselves.[1]

While the Roman Catholic emphasis would pick up on and
endorse many of the points that the former Archbishop of
Canterbury made on this occasion – after all, this is a passionate
insight into the spirituality of priesthood – nevertheless, its own
theology stresses the ontological status of priesthood rather
more than is usual in Anglicanism. What does this mean in
practice? I am part of the generation which was brought up to
know the Catholic Penny Catechism by heart. We knew
therefore that baptism conferred 'a mark or character upon the
soul', and that this was true for women as well as men. That is
to to say that it affected your very being. So too with ordination
to the priesthood – though this, we were told, was only possible
for men. Still, it was gratifying to know that women are able to
undergo ontological change, even if only at baptism. That was
one of the messages we learnt along with the text.

What becomes important for Catholic theology, though, is that the ordained priest is a mediator (*in persona Christi*). As the one who offers the sacrifice of the Mass, the priest is mediator between humanity and God. The Mass is offered in union with Christ's perpetual offering to the Father. It makes effective the sacrifice of Jesus on Calvary. It is about life out of death. So, in any discussion of the place of women as priests in the Roman Catholic Church, we have to examine quite carefully what is meant by *in persona Christi*. The whole hierarchical symbolic structure from the Father to Christ to the world is held by some to make it unsatisfactory for women to be priests. This is the heart of the argument against the ordination of women.

But the Catholic tradition has not rested solely in this one place and it would be tragic to trap it there. These arguments against the ordination of women have been conducted in something of a vacuum. Christology has been treated as one discipline; Mariology as another. Yet Mary was at the cross as well as at the cradle. The cover of this book shows an extraordinary image, a wonderful representation of Mary from Ravenna. She stands exalted in a deep blue chasuble, with a stole around her neck. She is surrounded by gold mosaic relief, her hands raised in supplication and offering. This too is part of the Catholic tradition and we ignore it at our peril. For you do not have to look very far to find suitable imagery about the place of Mary which might make a new symbolic ordering of reality more appropriate. Here the flow would go something like this: the Word of God is conceived in a woman's body (and without male intervention) and brought forth to save. There are Catholic models available for the ordination question to be resolved in favour of women and not against them.

In conclusion, the arguments which this book examines can be summarized as follows:

- the ordination of women to the priesthood is the logical conclusion of all the recent work of Catholic theology about women and, in particular, about the holiness of all the baptized. It is not an aberration from what the Church teaches but rather a fulfilment of it;

- the tradition can be appropriately developed to encompass women's ordination as the key building blocks are already in place;
- not to ordain women would now be to compromise the Catholicity of the Church.

These questions must be examined if this book is to succeed in its purpose of offering the kind of connections which will effect reconciliation and a new way forward. That is why it has a glorious image of Mary, the mother of God, on its front cover.

NOTE

1 Hansard, Parliamentary Debates (1993), House of Lords Official Report, 549, 194, col. 1017.

I completed this book early in 1994 and it was already being set before the publication of the Apostolic Letter of His Holiness Pope John Paul II on Reserving Priestly Ordination to Men Alone (22 May 1994). In the event the publishers have kindly agreed to carry the full text of this letter as an appendix.

1

From Lady altars to alternatives for women

This book begins appropriately on a train, because it is a book about a journey. My fellow travellers include a silent young man in a blazer who sits opposite me and who has just taken out his passport to gaze marvelling at his own photo. On the other side of the aisle there are two travel agents. At first their conversation maddened me because it seemed so inconsequential. But then they began to talk about computers and the effects of computerization on their industry. The more senior of the two, a woman, hazarded a guess that before too long it would be possible to go into a supermarket and buy your international travel along with your groceries, at the flash of a plastic card, using self-operating buttons with an electronic pen. Here is your departure point, here is your destination. Mark them on the electronic map, choose your method of transport and hey presto, here are your tickets. So much for the services of travel agents.

Her colleague, a younger man, commented nervously 'Well, it won't happen in our lifetime'. That is when I wanted to intervene. To lean across and say 'Oh but yes, it will. And that's what I'm doing on this train, I'm making a journey in space, but also one in time. I'm going back to the place where once I thought like you. But I do so now as an alien, an explorer in search of the world of my lost certainties. And while the planet I come from is not one governed by computers or machines, in many respects it is run by them. It's not an unpleasant, hostile place, though it could easily become so. It's one which is in search of its own humanity; a world which stands in front of a locked door and which has suddenly detected the keyhole to this door. Now it is searching for the key to this locked door and, amongst those which present themselves, is a key which is called the ordination of women to the priesthood in the Catholic tradition. It is one which some people believe must be used if we are to open the Catholic heritage to a new generation.'

So, where am I travelling and why? I am on my way to Birmingham, to visit the Oratory Church where I was baptized. The walk from number 38 Highfield Road where I was born takes three minutes. It's a walk I made Sunday by Sunday – and often on weekdays too – as a child, passing the blue plaque on the other side of the street which marks the house where Tolkien the novelist lived from 1910 to 1911, the one on the Italianate front of the Oratory itself, which tells you that John Henry Newman lived here from 1852 to 1890, and so through the cool shade of its covered garden to the church door.

It's eleven o'clock in the morning. The July sunshine falls directly onto the high altar as I enter the church. I haven't worshipped here since I was eight, but I recognize the smell of the church instantly. It is, of course, quite beautiful, like the smell of an old book, the smell of the secrets of history. The church looks immaculate. It has recently been restored and is ordered and adorned for the glory of God. I make my way to the font where Father Dennis Shiel baptized me. He had married my grandparents and my parents and baptized us four children. He is my living link with Cardinal Newman, because he was the last novice whom Newman admitted into the Oratory community before his death in 1890.

It is a handsome marble font, with a fine statue of John the Baptist on the top of its carved wooden lid. This overtly Christian imagery is matched by something less restrained in the marble base of the font, seed pods which are bursting with energy and life. My Baby Book records that my very first outing was to the Oratory in the car, very soon after I was born. I wonder which I looked most like. Not the gaunt wooden John the Baptist I fancy, more like the swollen marble seed pods I fear.

If I write with a kind of exaltation about this kind of Catholic world I do so knowingly. It is – it was – a glorious world, an inclusive world in which everything made sense. It was a world in which everyone and everything had its place. Now, though, the sun has gone in, literally shifted away from the windows as I sit here with my notebook and thoughts, and also metaphorically as well. Nothing in the church shines any more. Who has touched the hem of Jesus' garment, that life has gone out from him? Who has sought healing, and what was our wound?

So I move restlessly away from the rows of chairs at the back of the church where the font stands. I walk up the left-hand aisle, past the altars dedicated to the Sts Thomas More and John Fisher, to the glorious dead young men who fell in the Great War, to St Athanasius, and then find myself before the Lady altar. I prayed here fervently as a child. And when I look at it now I can see why. This is English ornate at its most restrained, a soft coral, grey and green marble altar with a handsome silver lantern hanging before it. If you raise your eyes you can see the Latin inscription, *Maria immaculata in coelum gloriose assumpta*. Yet the central statue shows rather a comforting and not a particularly heavenly Mary. She stands in a red dress with a blue and gold cloak, her hand protectively around baby Jesus who is perched on a globe – or is it an apple – at her right side. A snake curls its way to defeat, its head crushed under Mary's right foot. When I was a child this statue told me all I needed to know about the proper role and proper dignity of women. Messages about God's choice of women, about the ambiguity of our fallen state and about the path to redemption which was offered through motherhood were displayed here before me.

This teaching was endorsed by everything I heard from the sanctuary, where priests and servers moved about in elaborate liturgical rhythms, going now to the epistle and now to the gospel side of the altar. The celebrant still faces away from the people in the Birmingham Oratory. A whole theology is cast in stone in the way the sanctuary is ordered. This is – that was – a theology which totally precluded questions about the ordination of women.

A final comment before I leave this church. There was a clue here that it might not always be so. To the right of the Lady altar, perched high in the air is a statue of St Cecilia. Unlike Mary she is a tall slender figure, dressed in a full-length red robe with a simple gold surplice over it. She holds a hand organ and is crowned with a martyr's garland of red and white flowers. She has no child, no snake, no husband but, as patron of music, she has a voice. Right now I seek to sing with her voice and to learn what her song may be.

As I go out from the church other people begin to move into it. A man has come in with a metal bucket and an old floor cloth. He is washing down the centre aisle. An elderly woman in a green woollen coat with a furry hat well pulled forward has stopped to chat with him and then, in an otherwise empty building, squeezed past me to sit two seats along and say her rosary. Now as I leave, there are four other women, lighting candles to their favourite saints, sitting, kneeling, standing in the house of the Lord. So while a man cleans this oratory to God, women use it as a place of consolation and prayer. Nothing I write in this book is intended to judge these women or that man. I merely hold up a mirror to them and look in it myself in order to learn from the images it throws back to me.

Outside in the sunlight I walk past the stones set in the side of the covered pathway that leads on to the street. They bear the names of eminent Oratorian Fathers. So, Newman is there, and Ambrose St John and others of his early companions. And so too is Father Dennis, to my great satisfaction: *Orate pro anima Patris Dionysii Florentii Sheil, annis LXXII in cong. completis, obiit die VIII Jun MCMLXII aet XCVI*. So, in the year in which I was going into the Lower Sixth, Father Dennis died at the age of 96 after 72 years as an Oratorian. He had been 24 when he joined Newman's community. I was 16 and would join Mary Ward's on leaving school. What I could not have anticipated was the fact that these two sets of experiences would be separated by theological changes which would transform everything in the Catholic imagination. The world into which he baptized me in 1947 was closer to that of 1890 than the one in which he died in 1962. Because by 1962 the Second Vatican Council was under way, and nothing would ever be the same again.

So what did I learn on my pilgrimage to Birmingham? On reflection I find that I was offered certain insights into the way in which the world represented by the Oratory church both then and now is ordered. 'Then' means in the early 1950s when I worshipped there as a child. 'Now' means something very similar to then, because this is a church which has changed very little. That is why I knew that it would open important secrets to me when I went to visit and pray there. This was an ordered world, one in which women were offered certain spiritual values and truths which nurtured a deep life of faith. I noticed certain of them on my pilgrimage to Birmingham. Firstly, this was a church in which women belonged as by right. We did not have to negotiate our place; it was given to us. We did not have to invent ways in which to pray; these were already there. We did not have to worry about the extent to which we were represented in the church; the iconography held our image up to all. Unlike the young man in his blazer travelling on a train, we did not have to keep sneaking glimpses at any passport photos. We existed and fitted and belonged. What we heard, too, in church included us, along with what we saw. The language was as inclusive as it was exclusive. That is to say, the services were in Latin. Everyone knew that the words used meant everyone. The only time I heard exclusive language as a child was on the feast of the Ascension. *Viri Galilaei*, the Introit began. 'Oh ye men of Galilee, why do you stand gazing into heaven?' As I saw it, that remark was addressed to the men and so was accurately rendered.

So why could this world not go on for ever? The story of the woman with the haemorrhage in Mark 5.21–43 provides me with an answer. This is why I ask 'Who has touched the hem of Jesus' garment, that life has gone out from him? Who has sought healing, and what was our wound?' For the social, political and economic world of Edgbaston Catholicism was a world which favoured some and ignored others. It was a world which ordered society to the advantage of some and disadvantage of others. A wounded world which, I now realize, sought our healing. The gospel story tells us that a crowd had gathered around Jesus to hear his teaching. On this occasion it came to them not in words but in a series of actions. For Jesus goes with Jairus, the ruler of the synagogue, to see his 12-year-old child, a beloved daughter who lies dying. The crowd moves with him, pushing and shoving their way towards Jairus' home, towards an insight into the condition of women.

The adult woman in this story hides in shame. For twelve years she has been an outcast from the social and emotional life of her village. The law holds her up as an object both of pity and of contempt. No wonder the 12-year-old girl might be defensive about growing up as a woman; the nameless outcast woman must have been a frightening reminder to her of the primeval fear we all have of blood. It is a mysterious force, full of energy and so of threat. The woman with the haemorrhage who bleeds without dying becomes a target for our fears. No wonder taboo laws were so strong in 'primitive' societies.

Jesus can heal her. Indeed he does heal her. He restores her body's integrity but equally her good name. He calls her 'daughter', reminding her of her inalienable rights as a child of God. He commends her faith and her faithfulness. He gives her peace and frees her from her pain.

Such peace and freedom were offered to the Roman Catholic Church by the Second Vatican Council. The Council reordered the Roman Catholic imagination by reminding everyone of the fullness of their baptismal call. It spoke with a new voice and with new enthusiasm about discerning the signs of the times. In both these ways, more than in any others, it brought change right into the centre of the believing community, just as Jesus preached change by enacting change.

For suddenly the Church began to talk in a totally new way about baptism. The emphasis was no longer on the washing away of original sin. Instead we began to hear about the 'universal call to holiness of all the baptized'. In virtue of baptism every Christian forms part of the 'A team'. There is

no longer a 'B team' (that is the one to which people who were
not nuns or priests used to belong). The images of separation
and isolation and perfection which had informed the
stonework and furnishings of the Birmingham Oratory began
to fade from my memory.

The trickle-down effect of these changes took time to reach
the convent which I entered in 1964. But over the next twenty
years I was to see profound changes. The nuns took off their
habits and moved into ordinary clothes and ordinary streets.
They began to notice that their neighbours fought and
quarrelled; that there were questions about domestic and
other kinds of violence living on their very doorsteps. They
began to watch more telly and read beyond the statutory
broadsheet which had thumped its way onto every convent
doormat in the land. They began to visit their own homes and
families more regularly and to see that in so-called 'good'
families like their own, people were making up their own
minds about papal teaching on birth control and allied topics.

They began to leave the convent in droves. At its heyday,
in 1962, there were 185,000 women religious in the United
States alone. Nowadays there are 110,000. Those who
stayed had to do some serious rethinking. The universal
call to holiness of all the baptized means that everyone
receives the same call, the call to be human and the call to
be holy. There are many different answers to this call and
'different from' does not mean 'better than'. Images of
perfection had to go. The shiny bright nun bit the dust. In
her place her slightly bedraggled and decidedly more
ordinary sister emerged and began the long and difficult
task of renewal. In a word, nuns suddenly entered the
mainstream of Roman Catholic thinking; they too began to
develop. And the development they underwent was a kind
of microcosm of the way the whole Church was going.
What is important to notice though is that up until this
moment they had been the 'sacred vessel of election' in
which the sense of vocation for women had been held in
trust in the Catholic tradition. If their sense of vocation and
role were going through a series of important changes, then
something of great significance was happening. It was not
simply that the nuns were running out of steam or being

unfaithful. Some new thing was coming into existence, and that meant the dismantling of the old.

The other insight which has transformed the Church's life since the Council, and one which is still working its way through our thinking is one which is captured by another of its catchphrases. As well as the universal call to holiness of all the baptized, a new buzz phrase entered our vocabulary. The Church exhorted us to listen to 'the signs of the times'. That looked harmless enough at first. Then a further question had to be faced, 'Yes, but whose signs?' This sounds so obvious and simple that I believe we have yet to see how dramatic its effects will be. Suddenly the words secular and worldly cannot be used with their old meanings.

An example. The present-day debate about the place of women in Church and society has its origins in a secular movement, the suffragettes, it is said. As it gains in strength, and women and men begin to talk more generally about the need for greater visibility of women, how do the Churches react? As women talk openly about vocations to the priesthood, how are we to understand what this means? The old language of condemnation and dismissal no longer works. We are talking about a sign of the times and this requires careful discernment rather than outright dismissal. The Church is committed to development and this means that it will be sustained only by what Newman called 'living ideas'. In the meantime plenty of other church teaching since *Rerum Novarum* a hundred years ago has spoken with passion about human dignity in general and the dignity of women in particular. The tide is on the turn and we ourselves with it. Present-day Roman Catholic ascetism seeks the liberation of the human person, a growth and development in self-acceptance which mirror and echo the divine acceptance.

There are hazards of course, and it would be naïve not to remember them. Certainly many of the nuns fell into them during the 1970s and 1980s. A preoccupation with personal growth can become self-absorbed and self-obsessed. Sensitivity-awareness raising and community discernment processes replaced the Rosary and Benediction. In this country Melvyn Matthews, the director of Ammerdown, noted in *The Tablet* that courses he offered on personal development were inevitably oversubscribed whereas those he offered on social problems folded through lack of interest. How are we to read this? As a condemnation of personal growth? Or as a sad indictment of the personal neglect which had characterized religious life up to that time? An experience from the world of commerce offers the same paradox, for over the period in question a revolution took place in all our thinking. Experience became privatized, salvation was to be tailor made. And nothing catches it so compellingly as the image of 'pick and mix' sweeties. The statutory quarter-ounce bag of lemon sherbets or bag of toffees was replaced by personalized, even designer sweet-shopping. Anyone could go into a department store, pick up a shovel at the sweet counter and begin to pick and mix the privatized sweetie bag of their choice. Is this a good thing or a bad thing? The exercise of choice and desire had been withheld from many women in the Church. Now we were experiencing desire and the strength of personal calls to renewal. Of course this could be dismissed as self-indulgence – greed at the candy counter – but I would be inclined to view it more objectively. Namely as a somewhat desperate attempt to achieve a modicum of humanity after years or even centuries of a crippling abnegation of self.

This is, of course, a particularly Catholic problem. I now recognize the possibility of discovering a sounder spirituality in sources well removed from our own times or even from Roman Catholicism. I recognize it though because it is familiar to me from what I know of the religious life at its best as a life of dedication and service. So I note something written by Evangeline Booth. The daughter of Catherine and William Booth, she became the worldwide General of the Salvation Army in 1934.

Many people think that the women of the Salvation Army are lassies who, in the main, spend their time and energies on waving the tambourine and shouting their 'Hallelujahs'. During the war, our girls achieved a reputation scarcely less embarrassing. It was supposed that their whole energies were devoted to serving out the doughnuts to the boys in the trenches and gaily welcoming bombardment as a short cut to glory.

Of the courage of our women officers, I would be the last person in the whole world to utter a word of depreciation. 'Tis conscience that makes cowards of us all, and if shell fire no longer alarms, it is because hell fire has lost its terrors.

But death and danger had not been the only trial of these women's faith. They had faced dirt, they had handled disease, they had not flinched before uttermost degradation, they had not been dismayed by the most awful defacements of God's image imprinted on our race; there is no depth of misery, of despair, of iniquity that is concealed from the steady eyes of the women of the Salvation Army.[1]

The commitment to restore the divine image to completion by having both women and men officers is echoed here in the work of the Army, a fearless commitment to healing the 'defacements of God's image imprinted on our race'. I recognize the same dedication and generosity, the same conviction that ours is a social gospel in the measured writing of Isabella Gilmore who worked to restore the deaconess order in the Anglican Church.

There are certain gifts natural and acquired, which are necessary if the work is to be done efficiently. We want women whose good natural capabilities have been improved by education, who can bring the habit of observation and the quickness of the cultivated eye and hand to the work, and whose health and strength are vigorous enough to meet the demands of a busy life. Women who realize that a gentle-woman can undertake the most menial duties, sweep a room, cook a meal, attend to a patient in the most loathesome state of neglect if need be, turn her hand to any work that meets her in the miserable rooms and degraded surroundings of the purlieus of London, should her lot be cast there, and yet feel that she is in her right place, that such service is honourable and dignified beyond expression, for it is a humble following of him who came not to be ministered unto but to minister. We want in fact the highest type of woman for the office.[2]

The original versions of these two texts were published in 1930 and 1962 respectively. They mark a sea change in the self-understanding of women, one which would of necessity be mirrored in the Roman Catholic community although it had been pioneered outside of it.

And so the unimaginable was about to become imaginable. Mine would be the first generation of Roman Catholic women to ask questions about our proper role and proper dignity. We were to discover that the Second Vatican Council would require this of us. And we would turn for inspiration both to the traditional image of the Virgin Mary and also to other ones. Like St Cecilia, for instance, and the other great women who discovered the authority that goes with having a voice. No wonder she caught my eye when I went back to stand at the Lady altar of my youth; no wonder it was her surplice which I felt as though I were seeing for the first time. No wonder that, in time, I would also rediscover other majestic images like the praying figure of Mary from the Archiepiscopal Chapel at Ravenna, the mother of God decked out in blue and gold.

NOTES

1   E. Booth, *Woman* (New York: Fleming H. Revell, 1930), pp. 28–9.
2   J. Grierson, *Isabella Gilmore* (London: SPCK, 1962), pp. 220–1.

2

Joy, hopes, griefs, anxieties

The joys and the hopes, the griefs and the anxieties of the men of this age, especially those who are poor or in any way afflicted, these too are the joys and hopes, the griefs and anxieties of the followers of Christ. Indeed nothing genuinely human fails to raise an echo in their hearts. For theirs is a community composed of men. United in Christ, they are led by the Holy Spirit in their journey to the kingdom of their Father and they have welcomed the news of salvation which is meant for every man. That is why this community realizes that it is truly and intimately linked with mankind and its history.[1]

The first line of this quotation is one of the most haunting written in the twentieth century. All our joys, hopes, griefs and anxieties find here a place where they may go, a place where they will be recognized and greeted as part of the Christian enterprise and not as some deviation from it. That is how I heard these words from *Gaudium et Spes* when I first read this document from Vatican II. Yet nowdays – nearly thirty years on – the message is an ambiguous one, because what I have written there no longer sounds quite right. Vatican II maybe meant everyone. But the text actually talks about men. Now you could argue that this is a quibble, that men meant men and women in 1966 – and indeed that it still does. But if history is truly our judge, then it must be conceded that men have done better out of this construct than women have done.

Nothing indicates more clearly to me the exact nature of the dilemma experienced by many Catholic women at the moment, whether or not we have vocations to the priesthood. At the time I felt nothing but the joys and hopes of which the Council Fathers wrote; nowadays I have to meet the griefs and anxieties too as these are increasingly voiced by women. At the time we experienced some kind of invitation. This was about taking the risk of being ourselves, about daring to name our true identity before God, including the calls we believed we heard.

So Vatican II promised women the most inspiring agenda imaginable, one which said that our joys and hopes, griefs and anxieties are legitimate. Only with the process of time has it proved to be otherwise. A subtle form of invisibility has fallen back into place; the invitation has been withdrawn. So it has been hard for women to hang on to the hope which the Council held out to us. The major teaching was given to everyone, but the small print revealed thinking which has been slower to emerge and which has come to dominate post-conciliar thinking. Ideology and theology began to go separate ways. As it happens, by the 1990s, it is precisely this compromise which is revisited by the debate about the ordination of women in the Catholic Church.

The upfront teaching, as I have indicated, was glorious. It set my generation on fire. We felt that we belonged in some objective and energized sense, not simply because we knew the culture backwards. We were no longer to be in the background, faithfully doing what we had been persuaded were the vital bits, namely the praying and the listening. From now on we would contribute, giving as well as receiving, actors in the drama of salvation, rather than passive recipients. This was confirmed when the Mass went from Latin into English. Up until that time individual girls at my school had 'answered' Mass; that is to say, that, from the Lower Fifth up, if you were good enough at the Latin you sat in the front row on the left and said the responses to the priest. Like some kind of pretend altar boy, only with a voice rather than a body. No one could see you, they just heard you if they chose to listen. Now we had not simply English Mass, but dialogue Mass too. Not simply one girl but a whole chapel full of girls could be the people of God, an articulate strong voice for the divine service. Change could happen and happen quickly. What was in order at the beginning of the year, or even of the school term, was out of order by the end. It was not simply that the Pope got down from his big portable chair, nor that we received communion in the hand or answered Mass in English. It was that these things happened quickly and without dissent. Authority took sides. And it came out on my side. So I loved it.

But there was another side to the story, and gradually I began to hear about that too. I found it hard to believe my mother's account of a visit to see her cousin in France. I knew that my grandmother had once belonged to the Petite Église, a Jansenist group. But I had no idea that the same underbelly of rumblings still went on. Till my mother came home from Nice and told me that the priest had slapped her hands away when she had put them out to receive communion. Along with the sense of glory, I soon realized, there came a sense of betrayal. Some Catholics resented the changes and could not move with them. The most famous name is, of course, that of Monseigneur Lefebvre.

Sadly because the dissent was so reactionary it was impossible to listen to it. A more moderate voice would have made a useful contribution and enabled a better dialogue between the best of the old and the best of the new. So much for lessons learnt after the event. Important lessons to learn, however, especially nowadays when polarization is again the order of the day. When people disagree so passionately (as they do, for instance, over ordination) it becomes hard to remember that minorities have rights, and that we ignore them at our peril. After all, new minority groups appear all the time which carry bits of the Christian message on behalf of us all, however fragmented these may be in form. Vatican II taught us to listen and to discern, not to despise or to dismiss.

So what did the Council teach about women? What in its teaching offered so much joy and hope yet, in the event, subtly failed to deliver?

We were ready for Vatican II. We responded generously to its texts. We welcomed the official version and also the Grail translations which made its insights accessible in ordinary but rather well-written English. It produced teaching which recognized both the emergence of the 'woman question' and also the gifts of women. We were not treated as a problem which has to be dealt with, but as people who may actively contribute to the life of Church and society at home, local, parish, national and international level. This was an enormously important stance to take. At the present time, the 'woman question' – like the issue of ordination – is often presented as though it were an enormous burden for the Church, rather than an opportunity to recognize the apostolic gifts of women.

> The laity carry out their manifold apostolate both in the Church and in the world. In both areas there exists a variety of opportunities for apostolic activity. We wish to list here the more important fields of action: namely, church communities, the family, youth, the social milieu, and national and international affairs. Since in our own times women have an ever more active share in the whole life of society, it is very important that they participate more widely also in the various fields of the Church's apostolate.[2]

This decree came into effect on 29 June 1966. That year Mrs Indira Gandhi became Prime Minister of India; Elizabeth Taylor starred in *Who's Afraid of Virginia Woolf?*; the Beatles sang of 'Eleanor Rigby'; and Elizabeth Arden died.

The active base of women in society was indeed in some kind of melting pot and the Council's decree offered hope as well as a promise. I was a novice at the time; being put through the series of hoops which masqueraded as useful training for the religious life before the Council's teaching made any real impact. No wonder I experienced its message as wholly benign and beneficial. This document in particular talked about formation and training, stressing that 'those who have the obligation for Christian education also have the duty to provide for formation in the apostolate'. Lay training was about to become the order of the day; and it was not biased in favour either of women or of men. There was no tag attached about ordination.

Elsewhere the same message about the impact of women in public life had been conveyed by a paragraph which at first sight looked quite healthy. As I read it now I think about my contemporaries: the women who had been educated alongside me by nuns who did not simply encourage us to do well, but to do our very best. A recent book, *The Best Type of Girl*, gives a generous accolade to the school we had all attended. It reminds me that we absorbed generous views along with the landscape of North Dorset. So that I have broader questions in my mind when I read passages such as this one:

> Women are now employed in almost every area of life. It is appropriate that they should be able to assume their full proper role in accordance with their own nature. Everyone should acknowledge and favour the proper and necessary participation of women in cultural life.[3]

For here we read of the 'full proper role' of women, something which is deemed to be 'in accordance with their own nature'. So that what was given when the Council Fathers taught that 'everyone should acknowledge and favour' that 'the participation of women is necessary in cultural life' is somehow retracted when what they favoured has to be *proper*. For what is proper, what is the full proper role of women? And how does it accord with this thing called 'their own nature'? How helpful would my contemporaries have found those words as they began to wrestle with the options their good Catholic education had opened up to them? In our final year at school we had listened to careers talks given by people from the caring professions. But we had heard other scripts as well, from our brothers for example, whose aspirations we somehow knew we could match. All this talk about the proper role and true nature of women was to become vaguely disquieting. Was it really for this that we had all stood outside on the day the Council had opened and prayed for the Holy Spirit to descend on the Council Fathers, as we listened to the clanging of every bell on the school campus? Was it for this that Sts Michael and Gabriel and all our other bells rang out in a cacophony of sound?

I realize now that when we were looking for insight we had a new source along with the Council documents. For we were the first generation of young Catholic women who were actively encouraged to turn to the Bible. We knew the gospels backwards of course, because we had studied them for O level. Indeed we had been helped to pray with gospel texts; but we did so in a muted kind of way, without realizing that the ones about women were more about us than the ones about men were. Yet nowadays when I search for a mirror to try to look at this question of woman's nature and what the idea of 'proper' might mean, I can no longer read the Bible in that naïve way. So I turn consciously to the story of an improper woman from the Gospel. At the well of Samaria in John 4.1–26, an unnamed woman meets a Jesus who has no doubts about his mission to save her. She is part of, not apart from, the saving mysteries of human redemption. She belongs in the gospel story just as I was to find that I belonged. That is why Jesus demands openness and clarity from her.

For John is specific. The 'hour' at which Jesus meets this woman is the sixth hour, that is to say noontime. There can be no shadow or darkness here, only light. This is demonstrated by the way Jesus deals with the nameless woman. He does not threaten or bully her; he asks her for a drink of water. In doing so he invites her to cross a barrier, a series of barriers which image and mirror and echo each other. Boundaries between Jews and Samaritans, women and men, the poor and the rich, the strong and the weak. They are no longer to make each the shadow or dark side of the other. All are to come into the fullness of the light where their definitions of each other will be informed by mutual interchange and an exploration of what they have in common. That is why *Gaudium et Spes* jars as I reread it now. For the document goes on:

> Today it is more difficult than ever for a synthesis to be formed of the various branches of knowledge and the arts. For while the mass and the diversity of cultural factors are increasing, there is a decline in the individual man's ability to grasp and unify these elements. Thus the ideal of 'the universal man' is disappearing more and more. Nevertheless, it remains each man's duty to preserve a view of the whole human person, a view in which the values of intellect, will, conscience, and fraternity are pre-eminent. These values are all rooted in God the Creator and have been wonderfully restored and elevated in Christ.[4]

With hindsight we can say that it is not surprising that generalized ways of talking or thinking no longer worked. Because now we can see quite clearly that something normative but incomplete is being described in this passage: man as the pre-eminent repository of intellect, will and conscience, man whose pre-eminent way of relating is fraternity. And let's be quite clear about it, this time 'man' surely means 'men'. Texts such as this reveal that while on the one hand 'there is a decline in the individual man's ability to grasp and unify', nevertheless, on the other hand, this does not mean reaching out to others – women, for example – in order to get a more rounded view of what it might be to be human. Instead the doctrine of autonomy remains in place; aloneness is valued whereas community is not. And the result is a chilling piece of prose which says nothing about how people are to get on together.

To say that some human qualities, such as a well-developed emotional life, intuition, gentleness and so on are feminine qualities is not to claim that all women have these qualities in abundance. Far from it; many men have access to them too. But to list human qualities which draw uniquely from a list which is constructed as masculine, as *Gaudium et Spes* did here in 1965, is to do women a disservice by constraining them to invisibility. It is also to disallow such qualities as part of any fully human response. I realize now that an unspoken consequence of such a clear-cut ordering of reality is that women cannot possibly take up their place at the altar. They are too insubstantial to be there because they are excluded from intellect, will, conscience and fraternity.

But equally I am left wondering what the proper dignity of men might be, for the simple reason that a list of qualities like intellect, will, conscience and fraternity makes male normative. Yet this is never quite followed to its logical conclusion by spelling out the true nature of man. So I turn once more to what the Council Fathers wrote when they reflected on women and men and children:

> The family is a kind of school of deeper humanity. But if it is to achieve the full flowering of its life and mission, it needs the kindly communion of minds and the joint deliberation of spouses, as well as the painstaking cooperation of parents in the education of their children. The active presence of the father is highly beneficial to their formation. The children, especially the younger among them, need the care of their mother at home. This domestic role of hers must be safely preserved, though the legitimate social progress of women should not be underrated on that account.[5]

The initial definition is beautiful: 'the family is a kind of school of deeper humanity'. It leans on what St Benedict wrote when he described monastic life as a 'school of the Lord's service', namely a place of acceptance and growth. Moreover the text suggests that families have a mission as well as a life, that is to say that they exist in the public domain as well as in private. The problem comes when one considers who the teachers in this school shall be, and who will have access to the public mission and who to the private life of the family. Because here we have a hint of the 'proper dignity' of man. He is to be the active one, the hunter and the forager, while she is assigned the domestic role. For all its warm insights about the kindly communion, joint deliberation and painstaking co-operation – as well as the legitimate social progress of women – they remained trapped here in a world in which any aspiration to exist outside the magic construct as domestic mother is cut short. The woman whose proper role is spelt out in this passage should never aspire to listen to a vocation to the priesthood. Small children and hungry husbands are the only people who can ever turn to her for care.

So much, too, for the strange irony in the fact that the Council knew that 'People hounded by hunger call upon those better off. Where they have not yet won it, women claim for themselves an equity with men before the law and in fact.'[6]

Is there a glimmer of hope or is there an an additional twist in the way in which the *Constitution* spelled out so eloquently what this equity was meant to look like? How can the present-day hunger of women be met?

> Since all men possess a rational soul and are created in God's likeness, since they have the same nature and origin, have been redeemed by Christ, and enjoy the same divine calling and destiny, the basic equality of all must receive increasingly greater recognition.
>
> True, all men are not alike from the point of view of varying physical power and the diversity of intellectual and moral resources. Nevertheless, with respect to the fundamental rights of the person, every type of discrimination, whether social or cultural, whether based on sex, race, colour, social condition, language or religion, is to be overcome and eradicated as contrary to God's intent. For in truth it must still be regretted that fundamental personal rights are not yet being universally honoured. Such is the case of a woman who is denied the right and freedom to choose a husband, to embrace a state of life, or to acquire an education or cultural benefits equal to those recognized for men.[7]

Nowhere is it so clear as here that the Council did indeed offer hope to women, a hope that expressed what was given to all on account of baptismal calling and gift of discernment. What was hinted at was recognition. Even as the stereotypes were trotted out one more time – about 'varying physical

power and the diversity of intellectual and moral resources' –
what we were offered here was something visionary.
Something that went far beyond narrow ideas about the
proper role and proper dignity either of women or of men.
Something which might meet our hunger.

No wonder that, to many of my generation, Vatican II
marks such a turning point. What we read as we explored the
Council documents would lead us to say 'Yes, so far so good.
But there are other rights beyond choosing a husband. There
are other callings beyond the so-called states of life which are
presently open to us, callings to ordained ministry for
instance. And how can you defend our right and freedom to
acquire education and cultural benefits when you deny our
right and freedom to aspire to use these for the well-being of
the Church? By seeking out ordination, for instance. And
anyway, why do we have these rights? If we can be baptized,
why can we not be ordained? Let us at least talk about the
theological assumptions you're beginning to make?'

That, in a word, is the dilemma for present-day Roman
Catholic women. And lest anyone assume that what I am
writing about is simple or clear, let us also remember that
there are considerable numbers of women as well as men in
the Church who love the traditional roles assigned to them by
papal teaching about the proper dignity and role of women.
They can be threatened and become aggressive when
challenged, just as those who seek other roles for women can
be by their traditionalism. All the more reason then to explore
what else the Catholic Church, and particularly its
magisterium, has offered to the self-understanding of women
and men in the post-conciliar period.

Because, in the event, the justice agenda hinted at by words
like 'equity' would actually fail women. It raised the level of
their joys and hopes by giving them new aspirations but left
them with new griefs and anxieties. Vatican II produced a
generation of women who would aspire to be assimilated in
new ways into church life and to be ordained as priests. Yet
ironically it could not hear them talk about their vocations to
the priesthood while it continued to conduct the conversation

at the level of what is natural or proper or even, sadly, equitable. Only a new way of looking at women theologically would bring about true change. And of course the Council had produced a new wave of theologians. So there was hope. And there would be joy.

NOTES

1 *Pastoral Constitution on the Church in the Modern World*; from W. M. Abbott SJ (ed.), *The Documents of Vatican II* (New York: Guild Press/London: Geoffrey Chapman, 1966), pp. 299-300.
2 *Decree on the Apostolate of the Laity*; from Abbott, p. 500.
3 *Pastoral Constitution on the Church in the Modern World*, p. 267.
4 Ibid., p. 267.
5 Ibid., p. 257.
6 Ibid., p. 207.
7 Ibid., pp. 227–8.

3

The emerging sound of women's voices

In 1976 the world's first supersonic passenger service was launched with simultaneous departures of Concorde aeroplanes from Paris and London. That year too the Orient Express ended its Istanbul to Paris run. The old went out with the coming of the new. And, as the conversation of the travel agents at the beginning of this book reminded me, with the new would come undreamed of and unimagined futures. In church circles too, changes were underway, even if they came in less dramatic packaging. They too were about movement and sound, the emerging sound of women's voices. And they too heralded a new awareness.

1976 was also International Woman's Year and a cluster of papal documents were timed to come out then, including *Inter Insigniores*, a Declaration on the Admission of Women to the Ministerial Priesthood. Others followed which dealt with issues about women's sexuality. A third kind of official Catholic teaching around this time comes from a mix of sources. These mark out some interesting new territory and make an oblique kind of comment on the others. For here we begin to see new theological insights about the place and contribution of women to church life and a recognition of the gifts of apostolic women.

So, for an example of the first kind, the ones which coincided with International Woman's Year, I turn to a document from the Sacred Congregation for the Evangelization of Peoples, otherwise known as the Propaganda Fide. Entirely upbeat in tone, *The Role of Women in Evangelization* demonstrated where the ministry of women was flourishing.

> In the light of experience and in accordance with suggestions made by women evangelists themselves, the participation of women in the proclamation of the Good News can take many forms; one can but briefly enumerate them:
>
> Catechizing, both Catechumens and Christians
> Visiting families, the poor, the sick, outcasts
> Involvement in retreats and spirituality sessions
> Teaching religion, to the level of theology, in every capacity
> The mass media: press, radio, television.[1]

Women were to be consulted, to participate, and to be theologically literate. They were obviously fulfilling the traditional ministries of the corporal works of mercy, but now they were adding new spiritual ministries through involvement in retreats and spirituality. There was another new angle though, even where they exercised the most traditional of baptismal ministries. They were to go out, to visit families and the poor, sick and outcasts where these people were. Not simply expect them to turn up on their doorsteps. And then the final insight: that the media – that most extroverted of industries – offered quite extraordinary openings to the ministry of women.

I remember 1976 well. That year I made a retreat directed by a woman for the first time. The setting was spectacular, the Jesuit retreat house in the Dordogne in France, a dusty path down to the river, warm swims in the afternoons. The programme offered a week's seminar on the *Spiritual Exercises* of St Ignatius preceded by a week's retreat. My director had been a missionary in Japan and provincial superior of her religious congregation there. She wore a kimono and neat little slippers in the evenings. So what was happening to me?

I was being ministered to by someone like me, not someone unlike me. And that came as a shock. Because many of my unknown defences were dismantled. I say unknown because they were unknown to me. I had never previously realized the extent to which I had screened out unpalatable information from myself and from previous retreat directors. Yet the mirror into which I looked now threw back an image of someone like me, rather than unlike me. Up until then I had not realized how powerful a distortion of me ordinarily faced me and judged me and found me wanting.

When the retreat ended and the seminar began, it was conducted exclusively by men. My memory is of a particularly distinguished French Jesuit who gave luminary discourses and crunched indigestion tablets on the sly. At the time I made no connections; now I realize that my first impression of a directed retreat given by a woman marked 1976 off for me as a year of profound change.

Yet when I read the official version of what I had experienced I notice one discordant phrase in the document. The phrase which says that women should teach religion 'in every capacity' is not borne out by the facts. There had been one somewhat irregular liturgy at the retreat I remember, by candlelight and with a reading from Luke's Gospel instead of the eucharistic prayer, celebrated by the priests certainly, but with my nun director in evidence. But she was not there in 'every capacity', as she had not been the celebrant. Nor had she preached.

Inter Insigniores, a declaration on the Admission of Women to the Ministerial Priesthood, published four months later by the Sacred Congregation for the Doctrine of the Faith, laid out the ground rules. It has a pleasing title. One which does not start out to condemn (a declaration on the total unsuitability of women to come near the sanctuary, for instance), but rather one which seeks to examine the arguments. It began by describing the role of women in modern society and the Church, switched back to the Church's 'Constant Tradition' (more of this in Chapter 4), turned to the attitude of Christ, the practice of the Apostles and their 'Permanent Value', and then examined the ministerial priesthood in the light of the mystery of Christ, concluding with an inspiring treatment of the ministerial priesthood illustrated by the mystery of the Church.

When I first read documents such as these, I believed that the Church was offering me doctrinal insights which were invaluable for my growth in faith. *Inter Insigniores* reminded me that St Teresa of Avila had been declared a Doctor of the Universal Church (27 September 1970). From Teresa, as from my French woman retreat director, I learnt about the importance of intellectual rigour and valued it wherever I recognized it. After all it was she who reminded the Christian community about the kind of qualities we should seek out and admire in those who are to direct and teach us:

It is of great importance, then, that the director should be a prudent man – of sound understanding, I mean – and also an experienced one; if he is a learned man as well, that is a very great advantage. But if all these three qualities cannot be found in the same man, the first two are the more important, for it is always possible to find learned men to consult when necessary. I mean that learning is of little benefit to beginners, except in men of prayer. I do not mean that beginners should have no communication with learned men, for I should prefer spirituality to be unaccompanied by prayer than not to be founded upon the truth. Learning is a great thing, for it teaches those of us who have little knowledge, and gives us light, so that, when we are faced with the truth of holy scripture, we act as we should. From foolish devotions may God deliver us!

I want to explain myself further, for I seem to be getting involved in a great many subjects. I have always had this failing – that I cannot explain myself, as I have said, except at the cost of many words. A nun begins to practise prayer: if her director is a simpleton and gets the idea into his head, he will give her to understand that it is better for her to obey him than her superior, and he will do this without any evil intention, thinking he is right. Indeed, if he is not a religious, it will probably seem right to him. If he is dealing with a married woman, he will tell her it is better for her to be engaged in prayer when she has work to do in her home, although this may displease her husband: he cannot advise

her about arranging her time and work so that everything
is done as true Christianity demands. Not being
enlightened himself, he cannot enlighten others, even if he
tries. And although learning may not seem necessary for
this, my opinion has always been, and always will be, that
every Christian should try to consult some learned person,
if he can, and the more learned this person, the better.
Those who walk in the way of prayer have the greater need
of learning; and the more spiritual they are, the greater is
their need.[2]

What should have alarmed me, though, is something which
I discover now as I reread these documents, and especially
this one about women and priesthood. 'The Catholic Church
has never felt that priestly or episcopal ordination can be
validly conferred on women.'[3] In this sentence feelings are
validated. Yet further into the text they are discredited: 'It is
sometimes said and written in books and periodicals that
some women feel that they have a vocation to the
priesthood.'[4]

You are left wondering whose feelings are to be taken
seriously and whose rejected. The problem, as I now see it, is
that women who were engaged in precisely those ministries
which were commended by the Sacred Congregation for the
Evangelization of the Peoples, namely spiritual direction and
retreat work, as well as those who worked in the media, were
making new connections. They knew, because they were
reading the classical spiritual texts from the tradition, such as
the *Spiritual Exercises* of St Ignatius, that feelings cannot be
taken at face value, they cry out for discernment. In the world
of the arts and entertainment, moreover, women were
'feeling-literate', perfectly aware of the way in which rhetoric
– in words and images – can move and sway opinion. Teresa
of Avila talked about male spiritual directors; but she would
have wanted a fair line of argument from women and clearly
expected it from men. To validate the feelings of men at the
expense of the feelings of women is to make a nonsense of the
whole business of discernment.

Two further insights from this document will receive much
fuller treatment as the story line of this book develops. One is

about women as apostles or as disciples. These are texts which begin to argue against the apostolic vocation of women by saying that they may only be disciples of Jesus, never apostles. The other is about the priest as sign, 'a sign that must be perceptible and which the faithful must be able to recognize with ease'. They are the hub of the new theological argument about the place of woman at the altar.

The immediate postconciliar world produced a cluster of further teaching which is important because it was addressed to the self-understanding of women as sexual beings. The alphabet stretches from abortion, adoption and adultery; travels by way of birth-control, divorce and euthanasia; family planning, fertility and mixed marriage; to pornography, prostitution and the Women's Liberation Movement! No prizes for guessing which is the odd one out. And equally no prizes for noticing that this is a strangely impersonal list. These are topics which rapidly become problems. Rather than people who make up that strange, passionate, caring, desiring, questioning group we call Christian women and men.

Church teaching on human sexuality is an easy target. When I reread some of these documents I wonder at the plethora of social concerns which have sought public attention over the past twenty years. So much so that I choose to comment with broad stokes of the brush, rather than to nitpick about individual pieces of legislation or doctrine. Three things emerge. The overwhelming impression, as I say, is about the intensity with which the Church has engaged with these questions. This conveys a sense of concern and interest. But my second impression is of a widening gap. For during this period women have had control over their own fertility in ways unknown to previous generations. In my library of second-hand books about women, a collection which is nine hundred books strong, I have most of the works of Marie Stopes, the birth-control campaigner. The illustrations from her major opus *Contraception* remind me of nothing so much as the watercolours in first editions of Mrs Beeton's *Complete Cookery*. Mrs Beeton's are of pastry cutters and cream pumps. Marie Stopes are of contraceptive devices. Gleaming steel and crenellated rubber in contention.

Compared with which, the contraceptive pill would be an out-and-out winner. So that the odd one out in the list I gave above was not the Women's Liberation Movement; it was birth-control. What women did in practice moved further and further away from what they were being told to do. And so a split came into the way in which Catholic women thought.

The third impression I have on rereading these postconciliar texts relates even more directly to the concerns of those who wish to debate the ordination of women in the Catholic Church. Because what follows from overconcern with birth-control is a distressing tendency to equate women with their reproductive capacity as in 'I ovulate, therefore I am'. Can they, can't they? should they, shouldn't they? when, where and how? within or outside of what kind of normative relationships? How can one possibly have a cool and lucid conversation about women and ordination when the 'biology is destiny' tapes are playing at full volume?

And lest anyone think that this particular equation is something left over from the 1970s, I note that someone who wrote in to the BBC after a Radio 4 broadcast I had done for the *Today* programme's Thought for the Day slot – about Emmeline Pankhurst's birthday and the work of Christian suffragettes – took issue with me on precisely this question: 'If Sister Lavinia Byrne believes', she wrote, 'in living a full life, why does she renounce her primal, *God-given* function of motherhood by becoming a nun? So much more vital than having the vote.' The letter writer did not give her address which is a pity, because I would have liked to thank her for making my point so well for me.

Because of the primitive nature of some of the arguments used by this school of thought, I turn with some relief to fragmented and disparate texts from the postconciliar collection of writings. An example makes my point. In 1976 the Sacred Congregation for Religious and Secular Institutes issued a short text called *Quitte ton Pays*.[5] Directed at a

pressing problem, namely the responsibilities of professed
religious women for their elderly parents, it offered useful
pastoral guidelines. Religious congregations had to be
humane in the face of parental need. Leaving one's country
was not meant to mean leaving one's humanity: 'a sister
cannot be unconcerned about the situation of her parents'.
More than that, though, the decree was quite clear: religious
women were not to be first in the firing line when a pair of
hands were needed in the parental home. 'Religious are not
the only ones who have obligations towards their parents.' So
their brothers and sisters have responsibilities too. Replace
the word 'religious' by women and the word 'parents' by
children and you see some new thinking. Women are more
than the mothers of children, just as nuns are more than the
daughters of parents. Family relationships matter of course,
but they are not the beginning, middle and end of anyone's
self-understanding.

What I notice as I read further is that this analogy can be
applied across the board. Professed religious are women who
have deliberately chosen not to be described in terms of their
fertility or capacity for child nurture. Church teaching about
the nuns has had to take into account the autonomous, single
woman with her call from God. Indeed it has consciously
validated it, even though the Church has, on occasion, had a
problem with the calling and gifts of certain individual sisters.
So who is she most like, this autonomous single woman? The
Virgin Mary of the statue I knew as a child, or the singing
figure of St Cecilia in her red robe and golden surplice?

Or to use a Gospel analogy, Martha or Mary? The story of
these two sisters told in Luke 10.38–42 has often been used
as a way of making women feel guilty. Martha is the sensible
one who rolls up her sleeves and gets on with the dishes; Mary
has the kind word from Jesus, though, because she is quiet
and sits at his feet. The active woman is judged by the
contemplative; but equally the contemplative is condemned
by the active one. Or so the usual interpretation has gone.
Some contemporary scholars have suggested that this is not
really the correct focus for understanding this story. There is
an added dimension to it. Mary sits at the feet of Jesus and is
set free by him because she listens to him and learns from

him. In the Jewish tradition, to have someone sit at your feet was to accept that person as your student. Rabbis in particular trained their young aspirant colleagues by calling them to sit at their feet and learn the intricacies of the Law at first hand. Mary is scolded by Martha – and praised by Jesus – because she seeks to learn the wisdom of the new law from him, not because she is skipping the washing up.

Empowered with the wisdom she learns from Jesus, Mary will be able to choose when to work, when to pray, when to relax or celebrate, and when to study. She will have learnt discernment and will get the balance right. Contemplation and action are not set in opposition; true wisdom lies in doing everything we have to do contemplatively, that is to say, with the eye of faith.

So we should not be surprised when this contemplative eye of faith is brought to bear on the strands most commonly taken up by papal teaching during the years after the Council and then developed in a fully articulated sense in the document *Mulieris Dignitatem* of 1988. All the best themes are there: about the dignity and rights of women. But so too are the unhelpful ones about sexual stereotyping, alias the proper role of women; and even the more damning ones than that, namely about the true nature of woman. So that it has now become quite clear that the real question is a theological one; the justice agenda fails to make any real impact. Where a bid for justice makes an appeal to the emotions, a bid for theological integrity is directed at the mind. Those who distrust their emotions can easily deflect the claims of people who work for change. Whereas a new theological argument opens up the possibility of asking new questions. As I reread *Mulieris Dignitatem* I become conscious that what is now needed is a theology which takes account of contemporary sciences. Then we can all learn from the work done by people who study how human beings live and interact and reproduce and grow, as well as that done by people who have begun to read the Bible in new ways and teach something wholesome about the dignity of all human beings, made in the image and likeness of God.

I recognize a hunger for this work to be done. I see signs of it every time I open the newspapers. For there I read stories about the conflicting demands society makes on working women when we are expected to manage everything super-competently without ever feeling guilty about where we put the greater part of our energy. There I read stories about women who want to conceive, who cannot conceive; who want to adopt, who cannot adopt. Some of these women are too old, too young; too fat, too thin – or so we are told. All are cannon-fodder for a work-force which offers part-time employment while failing to guarantee pension rights and holidays; all are cast into oblivion when we forget about the many women whose home is their place of (unpaid) work. This is the generation which is most open to deliverance but equally to exploitation at the hand of the pharmaceutical companies, the image makers, the microwave salesperson; or therapists and analysts and crystal gazers. A generation of women who need to learn to say no or yes out of conviction, not because we are afraid, nor because we know no better.

But I see other signs too. Every time I preach, be it on the larger canvas of a Westminster Abbey or in a small south-coast parish church, I am met with the same reaction: 'It's so lovely to have a lady priest.' 'Thank you dear. You said just what I needed to hear.' Try as I may to explain that I am not a lady priest, that is not the point. What is being put into words, I believe, is a desire to hear theology made by women and to hear it from the sanctuary. That is why I am particularly delighted when I quote from the writings of earlier women preachers – such as Elsie Chamberlain, star of the BBC; Evangeline Booth, first woman General of the Salvation Army; Caroline Graveson, who delivered the Quakers' Swarthmore Lecture in 1937 – because my hunch is constantly being confirmed.

This hunch is that there is a genuine thirst for more to be said about the place of women in Church and society. And that does not mean more of the same. The old rhetoric no longer works. And women who are brave enough to say this should be encouraged and nurtured because they are calling the Christian Churches to new life and to new faith. And, above all, to a new theology. For that reason it is essential to identify how the Church names, who it names and why. That is why the next chapter must follow my hunch and find out what patterns of naming or theology-making are preserved in the Church's hidden tradition.

After all, it was 'the Church's constant tradition' which was the backbone of the arguments against ordination used in *Inter Insigniores*, despite the fact that 'the Pontifical Commission, when questioned on this matter by Paul VI, answered that, in their opinion, there was no valid biblical basis for opposing the ordination of women to the priesthood'.[6]

So what tradition are we talking about, and whose tradition? One which reveals 'the undeniable influence of prejudices unfavourable to women'?[7] Or one which recognizes and values the gifts and – above all – the call of apostolic women? Including the call to priesthood.

NOTES

1 Austin Flannery (ed.), *Vatican II: More Postconciliar Documents*, vol. II (New York: Costello Publishing Company Inc., 1982), p. 123.
2 Teresa of Jesus, *The Complete Works*, vol. 1, ed. E. A. Peers (London: Sheed & Ward, 1946), pp. 80–1.
3 Flannery, vol. II, p. 333.
4 Ibid., p. 342.
5 Ibid., pp. 203–8.
6 Elisabeth Behr-Sigel, '"The ordination of women: an ecumenical problem": a right to a reply', *Sobornost*, 15, 1 (March 1993), p. 25.
7 Flannery, vol. II, p. 333.

4

The hidden tradition

In 1989 I edited a collection of women's spiritual writings called *The Hidden Tradition*. Two years later I followed this with further work on nineteenth- and early twentieth-century missionary women, only this time I called it *The Hidden Journey*. A third volume is in the pipeline: *The Hidden Voice*. Unwittingly, as I have worked on each of these, I have had to ask an uncomfortable question: Was this material lost by accident or was it actively suppressed? And that would be by women as well as by men. In the words of the feminist slogan: Did Eve fall, or was she pushed? And were the women whose stories I was busy retrieving and bringing into the light the kind of apostolically gifted women whose voices the Churches desperately need to hear at the moment?

So what did my hidden women say and why?

I think, in recent times, of Maude Royden, the Anglican lay woman. She lectured in the Oxford University Extension Delegacy and devoted her energies to campaigning for women's suffrage and religious and ethical rights. Then came the call to preach. In the first instance she was asked to do so by her long-time clergy friend Hudson Shaw in South Luffenham, Rutlandshire. This was deeply controversial. Following that, invitations came from 'Labour churches, socialist churches, Brotherhood churches and ethical churches', according to her biographer, Sheila Fletcher.

The National Mission of Repentance and Hope was launched in 1914. A number of 'Archbishop's messengers' were to be appointed to preach and speak in churches up and down the country. Maude was an obvious candidate. The Bishop of London laid down the very restrictive conditions under which women were to be permitted to address congregations. He later withdrew all permission under pressure from the anti-women lobby.

In March 1917 she was invited to preach at the City Temple in its 'great white pulpit'. This was an important invitation – the City Temple was a kind of Nonconformist St Paul's. While it was bold for them to invite a woman, someone must have remembered that this was not a 'first': Catherine Booth had preached there in 1888. After some turmoil, Maude decided to accept. She was subsequently 'pulpit assistant' there until 1920.

Stories such as hers have almost vanished from the Christian imagination and from our theology making. Yet what Maude Royden spotted is still extraordinarily important. So, for instance, she could write:

> The Church will never believe that women have a religious message until some of them get, and take, the opportunity to prove that they have. My taking it in a Nonconformist church will ultimately lead, I believe, to other women being given it in the Church of England.[1]

And she was quick to notice how hard it is to take the opportunities which present themselves:

> Deacons, choristers, churchwardens, acolytes, servers and thurifers, even the takers-up of the collection, are almost exclusively men. If at any time not one male person can be found to collect, the priest does it himself, or, after a long and anxious pause, some woman, more unsexed than the rest, steps forward to perform this office. In one church I am told, it was the custom for collectors to take the collection up to the sanctuary rails, till the war compelled women to take the place of men, when they were directed to wait at the chancel steps. In another it was proposed to

elect a woman churchwarden, when the vicar vehemently protested on the ground that this would be a 'slur on the parish'. In another, the impossibility of getting any male youth to ring the sanctus-bell induced a lady to offer her services. After anxious thought the priest accepted her offer 'because the rope hung down behind a curtain, so no one would see her'.[2]

Catherine Booth had earlier asked what theological assumptions allow such treatment to go unquestioned:

> God having once spoken directly by woman, and man having once recognized her divine commission and obeyed it, on what ground is omnipotence to be restricted, or woman's spiritual labours ignored? Who shall dare say unto the Lord, 'What doest thou?' when he 'pours out his Spirit upon his handmaidens', or when it is poured out shall I render it null with impunity? If, indeed, there is 'in Christ Jesus neither male nor female', but in all touching his kingdom 'they are one', who shall dare thrust woman out of the Church's operations, or presume to put my candle which God has lighted under a bushel?[3]

There are other names in the tradition, of course: the Anglican, Isabella Gilmore; the Congregationalist minister, Hatty Baker; and Helen Barrett Montgomery, the North American Baptist. Their names read like a litany. These were women who began to make connections and to see that the light of Christ should indeed shine forth and not be placed under a bushel. They saw that there are curtains which hang down in people's minds as well as in their sanctuaries and that these should be drawn back. And nowadays, when Christian women meet together in ecumenical and other gatherings, these names are once again being used and talked about. The testimony of historical women is not treated as though it belongs only to one Church; increasingly the commonality of the hidden tradition of women is something which these groups deliberately choose to share. Being a woman becomes more important than being denominational. The historical evidence demonstrates clearly that women have suffered from prejudice and repression in all our Churches, so that what we have in common is held to be more important than what divides us.

At a press conference at the Palace of Westminster before the General Synod of the Church of England's debate about the ordination of women in 1992, I circulated some information about the ordination of women in the other Churches which are members of the Council of Churches for Britain and Ireland. It was a fairly matter-of-fact document, giving statistics about the number of ordained women ministers, with a list of organizations which campaign for and campaign against. It also included historical information, indicating when the Churches in question – Congregationalist (1916); Baptists (1918); the Presbyterian Church in Wales (1923); Church of Scotland (1968); Methodist (1974) – had ordained women. A rather florid North American reporter swept past me and said 'Not real priests'. Quite. But on one level that is not the point.

The hidden tradition is one which offers women solidarity. A chance of companionship and shared interest and concerns. So I am not surprised that a Salvation Army woman officer on a bus trip turned to me and said of her ministry 'I've been ordained for over twenty years'. She was explaining something to me in a way which would enable me to understand it. And also which would contextualize her experience and see it in a wider frame of reference. Equally I am not surprised when women students at a British theological college tell me that they resent the fact that the college authorities have only recently found the money (after several decades of women's ordination) to remove the male urinals from the ladies toilets on the third floor of their training college and to move the lights from over them to where they are actually needed.

I should add that the hidden tradition is one which is valued beyond the magic circle of ordained women. In 1993, BBC's *Woman's Hour* produced a quilt with squares depicting the contribution of women to public life. So Emily Wilding Davison and the suffragettes were there; the peace campaigners; the educationists; Amy Johnson, the aviator, and a host of other distinguished women – known as well as unknown. What surprised me was that, of the one hundred-plus quilted squares received by *Woman's Hour*, ten were about the ordination of women. And they are all there in the completed quilt. They make an extraordinarily powerful statement about what women value and where their energy is directed. No wonder that the quilt made by Ecumenical Women in the North East and hung in Durham Cathedral on 25 January 1992 had identified Catherine Booth and Maude Royden by name. As well as a host of other Christian women from all our traditions. No wonder that it had named the question of ordination as a theological hook, on which to hang a host of other issues.

That is why I am not surprised either when women who would either profess to be agnostic or not necessarily believers at all tell me that they were at Dean's Yard in Westminster on 11 November 1992. Or that they raised their glasses in London's wine bars after work when the news of the vote came through. 'It's not just about Anglican women; it's about all of us' was how a woman Rabbi friend put it to me. The *Sun*'s headline the next day maybe trivialized the event: VICARS IN KNICKERS, but what it communicated to me was the fact that something had been done which, for once, had real – and accessible – news value. Images from the BBC's televised reporting of the debate were carried on TV networks all over the world. People cared. And were prepared to show they did. They are the very people who have been bored and disinterested and ultimately disedified by the politicking and compromise which have followed that vote, as great thick clouds once again descend upon what it represented.

That is why I have been concerned to examine the mechanics of suppression in the work I have done editing the stories of earlier church women in the home and overseas missions. In the introduction to *The Hidden Journey*, I wrote:

The missionary women's story is subject to the same forms of suppression as those of the other women spiritual writers and theologians and mystics. At its best this suppression happens by accident because women's history is somehow deemed to be less important than that of men and so it fails to get told. And women themselves collude with this silence by not taking their experience sufficiently seriously, so not bothering to write it down. Or worse by keeping silent out of a warped desire to avoid vainglory.

At its worst an actual dynamic of suppression is operating. This means that what women were writing or talking about was not liked and so their access to the printed word was inhibited. Their books were printed in small numbers by publishers whose good will alone could not guarantee their survival. They are in limited supply nowadays, curiosities in second-hand book shops or cannon-fodder/space-fillers in charity and thrift shops. The major great histories of the missions published in this century virtually ignore them. Stephen Neill's 1963 *History of the Christian Missions* would be a case in point. But present-day histories are often just as well guarded. And so there is a reluctance to name the wives of the 'true greats' like David Livingstone – Mary (so frequently abandoned); or William Carey – Dorothy (who died from sheer misery); or Nicolaus von Zinzendorf – Erdmuth (who was deceived by her husband), just in case the truth should backfire and raise ugly questions about the extent to which a man's call to ministry should be exercised at the expense of his call to marriage.

Then there are questions raised by the very nature of the missionary women's ministry. When they took on the agenda of justice and began to question the cultural norms which meant that women's feet were tortured and bound in China, that widows were killed in India, that twin-children were slaughtered in Africa, that girl children were forced into prostitution and grown women into zenana harems, they challenged a world which had been established by men for the convenience and servicing of men, whatever their religious tradition. Islam, Hinduism, the African religions were judged and found wanting; but then so too was Christianity.

This was why the connections which the missionary women began to make made them a dangerous force within Christianity. The very freedom they professed to proclaim, the gospel message itself, turned round and hit them in the face and demanded that they too become accountable to the Lord of history. When they named the outrage they felt as they witnessed the violation of women's human rights, they raised difficult questions about the place of women in any society, including their own. When they called for change, they were demanding change for themselves as well. When they freed women by ensuring that they should have education, they challenged the entire social structure which, traditionally, had restricted it to men. In a most moving way the journey of the missionary women was a journey into freedom. They purported to bring a gospel of salvation; ironically, they found themselves receiving one.[4]

Books and stories are not the only medium for communicating history to us. This thesis was developed by the BBC's documentary series *Everyman* when examining the theme of the ordination of women in the week before the Church of England Synod's vote in November 1992. Here the medium was visual and so was the documentary evidence. The producer of this award-winning programme, Angela Tilby, used the title *The Hidden Tradition* and explored what evidence could be detected for the existence of women priests in the early Church.

The film was interesting for the simple reason that it came down neither on the side of the advocates of women priests nor of their opponents. Rather it showed what happens when we look at epigraphic and archaeological evidence. For we read it as we choose to read it. So a second-century fresco of seven figures intimately grouped around a table in the Catacomb of Priscilla in Rome will be described as men by some people, and as women by others. Those who claim that a symbolic system requires the representation of Jesus will see these figures as men, with one veiled woman amongst them. Indeed when the archaeologist Joseph Wilpert discovered this fresco in the nineteenth century he commissioned a water-colour reproduction of it. The artist who made a copy of this scene for the archives of the Pontifical Commission of Sacred

Archaeology actually firmed up the evidence by adding manly thighs and a beard to the figure closest to us and made sure the others looked like real men – bar the veiled figure of the real/proper/natural woman. When you see the primary evidence and then you see how it has been interpreted, you realize that you are in the presence of a massive agenda. And that the word 'hidden' is used advisedly of women in the tradition.

That is why the advocates of women's ordination, such as Mary Ann Rossi from the Women's Studies Department of the University of Wisconsin-Madison, make such elevated claims for the work they are doing:

> A recovery of women's full participation in early Christianity may be one means of confronting the persistent perception of women as subordinate in the Roman Catholic and Anglican Churches today. 'Images of the past that we carry within us do help to shape both our present and our future. A new set of images may have a liberating effect not only on scholars, with their specialized concerns, but also on the culture of which they are a part.'[5]

The author's quotation is from an article by John Gager on the origins of anti-Semitism. It serves as a useful reminder of the power of the visual evidence which is held up to us Sunday by Sunday as a picture of what a priest ought to look like. Only in darkened catacombs or, ambiguously, in mosaics are there images which tell a different story. I say ambiguously because Theodora the Woman Bishop, as she is known to her fans, from the east doorway of the Zeno chapel in the Basilica of St Praxedis in Rome divides opinion as much as she unites it. The word *episcopa* is written like a banner headline above her head. She is in exalted company, sharing a site with Sts Pudentiana and Praxedis and Mary the mother of Jesus. Yet her title is explained away by those who want to claim that the only reason for her being given such elevated status is that she must have been the mother of Pope Pascal who built the church.

Not only wall paintings and mosaics but also inscriptions have been uncovered over the past century. Fifteen of these so far, from ancient Gaul to Cappadocia, recall the work of women priests. Scholars who are pro-ordination drum up support for a fascinating reading of a comment ascribed to Athanasius in the fourth century. In a religious tract on the virtues of virginity he says that consecrated women may celebrate the breaking of bread together without the presence of a male priest: 'The holy virgins may bless the bread three times with the sign of the cross, give the thanksgiving and pray, for in the kingdom of heaven there is neither male nor female. All the women who were well received by the Lord achieved the rank of men' (*De Virginitate*: PG 28, col. 263). What happens this time is that the 'explainers away' tell us this is a rogue reading of Athanasius. The editor of *Patrologia Graeca* questions Athanasius' authorship of *De Virginitate*, despite the fact that St Jerome, a near contemporary, lists it in his *De Viris Illustribus*.

And the inscriptions? You would have thought a mid-fifth-century tomb discovered in 1876 in Tropaea provides unequivocal evidence: 'Sacred to her good memory Leta Presbytera lived 40 years, 8 months, 9 days, for whom her husband set up this tomb. She preceded him in peace on the day before the Ides of March.' 'Leta the Priest' is how the Latin inscription goes. But once again we are told that this should be read 'wife of'. Now this is evidence from southern Italy where there is another twist in the tale. Professor Giorgio Otranto is director of the Institute of Classical and Christian Studies at the University of Bari. In 1982 he published an evaluation of the letter which Pope Gelasius I (492-496) sent to the Bishops of southern Italy in 494. This letter has 27 decrees.

Four of the decrees were concerned with the presence of women in the context of the Christian communities: 12 concerns the consecration of virgins; 13 and 21 concern the prohibition against the veiling of widows; and 26, the most interesting to us, explicitly confronts the problem of the priesthood of women.

We have heard to our annoyance that divine affairs have come to such a low state that women are encouraged to officiate at the sacred altars, and to take part in all matters imputed to the offices of the male sex, to which they do not belong.[6]

Once again this has been treated as slippery evidence, with the assertion that southern Italy was more Greek than Roman and that pagan practices were more likely to have survived there than elsewhere. What Gelasius was dealing with, in the opinion of the opposition, were heretical groups.

I give Giorgio Otranto the last word:

I regret having to say this, but often historians, mostly Catholic historians, have shrugged off these bits of evidence and judge them as worthless, as though they had nothing to contribute to the total picture. There's been a repression, an attempt to put some historical sources to one side, at times out of conformity, at times out of prudence, out of acquiescence. I'm not saying out of bad faith, but it's certainly true that the prejudice which says women cannot perform priestly functions has allowed some evidence to be misinterpreted.[7]

Whose images work? Whose images are valid? In spite of some of the nagging contradictions presented by the evidence, what is interesting is to observe who supports which interpretation of it, and why. So some would see the ordained ministry of women in history as essentially heretical and deviant; whilst others would see it as a lost gift. Some want to tie it to pagan origins as a way of condemning it; whilst others are not quite so dismissive and would be interested to examine the pagan origins of all priesthood. Two ways of making theology clash over this question; one of which assumes that Christian revelation is fixed and unchanging, the other of which values process and disclosure.

So why is it important for this historical work to be done, if all it does is throw up inconclusive evidence? There are two main reasons I believe. Firstly in order to get away from the line of argument which demands ordination to the priesthood for women as a *right*. And secondly to set out the options for a new theology of priesthood. The hidden tradition reminds us that the active ministry of women in the Church has been veiled for far too long. Hatty Baker's *Woman in the Church* and Helen Barrett Montgomery's *Western Women in Eastern Lands* both date from 1911, before liberation theology had even been thought of. They sought priesthood for women but they also raised serious questions about all women, whether ordained or not. They knew that the same arguments against the active participation of women in church life were used by the anti-franchise lobby. Women were not to be given the vote for the very same reasons for which they could not be ordained. It was not proper or natural. It went against the divine order.

Chapters 2 and 3 have demonstrated the sense of exultation but also of betrayal that accompanies the preaching of a liberation and justice agenda for women. True conversion, the *metanoia* so beloved of the authors of Scripture, comes about when a less exciting but more far-reaching message is proclaimed, one which questions the way in which we construct our sense of what is proper or natural. What matters is our theology, not our sense of right and wrong. At its best the Second Vatican Council offered that very insight; that is why it produced women with priestly vocations. At its worst it offered an uncritical treatment of what the divine order might be; that is why it produced disgruntled women who felt supported neither in their roles in the home nor as they faced conflicting demands in the world of work.

So where was help to come from? The hidden tradition, recalled in this chapter, reminds us that there was a rescueable and recoverable past. And what about the future? Could the feminists race to the rescue? That is what the next two chapters must explore.

NOTES

1 Maude Royden to Miss A. M. Procter (20 March 1917); quoted by S. Fletcher, *Maude Royden: A Life* (Oxford: Basil Blackwell, 1989), p. 162.
2 Maude Royden, *Women and the Church of England* (London: George Allen & Unwin, 1916), pp. 8–9.
3 C. Booth, 'The call and ministry of women'; quoted by B. Booth, *Echoes and Memories* (London: Hodder and Stoughton, 1925).
4 Lavinia Byrne, *The Hidden Journey* (London: SPCK, 1993), pp. 10–11.
5 Mary Ann Rossi, 'Priesthood, precedent, and prejudice: on recovering the women priests of early Christianity', *Journal of Feminist Theology*, 7 (Spring 1991), pp. 73–94.
6 Giorgio Otranto, 'Note sul sacerdozio femminile nell'antichità in margine a una

testimonianza di Gelasio I', *Vetera Christianorum*, 19, tr. Mary Ann Rossi, pp. 341–60.
7   Interview for BBC *Everyman: The Hidden Tradition*, transmitted Sunday 8 November 1992.

5

The logic of feminism: being in the body, the natural and nature

Not only the hidden tradition but also new forms of a present-day tradition have been called into the arena by the present-day debate about the ordination of women to the priesthood in the Catholic Church. Forms of repression which Professor Otranto associates with the treatment of historical evidence are also at work nowadays.

I am told, for example, that the Church of England had no right to undertake to ordain women if it wishes to be taken seriously as a Church in the Catholic tradition. Which fails totally to square with the way in which my own Church has made theological changes over the past hundred years. I cannot remember it being explained that any serious consultation with Canterbury was in order when the doctrine of the Assumption of Our Lady into Heaven was declared, for instance. And why was there no similar difficulty when the Church of England introduced a General Synod, or ordained men to local pastoral charges rather than as priests of the whole Church? I am told that only a full Ecumenical Council – with full Orthodox participation – could bring about such a change in the Roman Catholic Church. And that is made to sound like something so utterly momentous that it will require a thousand years of preparation. And again that does not square with what I remember about the way in which Vatican II introduced changes which, at the time, I was told were of comparable importance for the Church. Mass in Latin became Mass in English. The disciplines which separated us from other Christians and forged our Catholic identity all went. No more fish on Friday; no more weddings in church porches for those who married 'out'; no more subtle superiority about being the only people who knew what we meant as we capped a profession of faith about being 'one, holy, catholic and apostolic' with prayers for the conversion of England.

When I first heard about feminist theology, I was a prime candidate for its insights. I was excited by the first feminist books I read. They claimed to offer the Churches something new which would retrieve theological discourse from the political minefield about what women should or should not do. Here at last was a clean slate, I believed. The problem, though, was that I was not a clean slate. Of necessity, I was something of a sceptic precisely because I am disillusioned with ideology in general, as well as with particular applications of it. Ideology cannot deliver the goods. And now, in the 1990s we realize that some of the rhetoric of feminism comes perilously close to ideology – as, indeed, does some of the rhetoric of those who oppose its insights. By ideology I mean glib answers, ones which line up 'correct' solutions.

In the search for a theological resolution to the question of women's place in the Church, it is therefore essential to evaluate the contribution feminism has made. Now, evaluate means listen to, learn from, but also question and critique. So what does it offer and what is the critique which it must undergo if it is to advance the cause of women?

Let me start with the up side. What is remarkable about feminism is that it has, virtually uniquely, brought fresh thinking to bear in a wide range of academic disciplines. It offers a series of insights which validate the experience of women. But, equally, it uses a new methodology, by inviting that experience into dialogue with the tradition. It has dared to challenge the most monolithic of contemporary idols: the world of psychology and, more than that, it advocates a new way of understanding how women and men are to relate to each other. It also requires of the Churches that we too overturn our idols. In this chapter I want to examine the logic of feminism, what it is. In the next I will ask how it works, that is to say, what its methodology is.

Having made such exalted claims for a dialogue with feminism I should add, of course, that there is a wide variety and range of feminist thinking and that feminists disagree amongst themselves about what works and what does not work. The word 'feminism' carries a variety of meanings, used by some as a badge of non-conformity, by some as a logical accompaniment to Christian commitment, and by others as a term of abuse and condemnation. All of which makes it very difficult to generalize.

Yet feminist theologians – both Christian and post-Christian – have said to women that our voices have been unheard for far too long. But that we are central, indeed mainstream to the Christian endeavour. Misogyny has adopted all sorts of unattractive disguises and, whether you call it patriarchy or paternalism, it has contained and used women as a servant class – made for, rather than with men. No wonder that feminism has emerged with such force in countries and nations whose story has been informed by the Christian story. It is, after all, a legitimate expression of what the Gospel both offers and promises. The first campaigners, the women who sought for the suffrage, or who set up church schools to educate women, knew that feminism is a product of Christianity. Present-day advocates see it as a liberation theology precisely because Jesus preached good news that would set people free. And not simply free up our voices. Feminism is not something which lives between the pages of a book. Some of its most creative energy has been released in dance and embroidery and song. The artefacts of feminism are highly celebratory, as is its best theology.

So what is this theology? One of its starting points is the place where women have been most grossly wounded by Christianity. The human body. Feminism does not simply like women as though this were somehow a nice idea, safe because cerebral. It goes deeper than that. And so it is not afraid of women's bodies, of whatever shape or size. Indeed it

is loud in its condemnation of the body/soul split which has
been so central to Christian orthodoxy. This is a split which
divided not only soul from body but also woman from man
because it was constructed along gender lines. Tertullian
taught that women were more gross and material, and
therefore that they were closer to death and decay. Men
meanwhile were finer, higher spirits. Growth and freedom,
for women, would only come about when they escaped from
the bonds of the flesh. And how would this be possible?

A whole range of neurotic behaviours were really the only
solution. Fasting and starvation, for instance, in order to
subdue the flesh and reduce it to the control of the mind. The
example of Catherine of Sienna would be a case in point.
Biographers have suggested that she used to vomit after
meals, a symptom we would associate with bulimia nervosa.
Rose of Lima is another example, sustained only by eating the
host at communion. When I was a child these stories were
told for my edification; at school I read 'spiritual reading'
books where the example of starving saints was held up for us
to copy. And when these women were not starving their
bodies into submission, they were punishing them in other
ways: disciplines, chains, whips were all part of Catholic
devotional piety, along with prayers about subjugation and,
hovering in the background, a sense that the ultimate goal
would be martyrdom – known euphemistically as dying for
the faith.

No wonder feminism was greeted with open arms because
it dared to question this ascetical conspiracy. In its place there
now comes the insight that women have a sense of
rootedness, a sense of being able to inhabit the human body
which is salvific. The flesh is no longer to be cut off from the
spirit, but rather our bodies – whether we are women or men
– are integral to our humanity, and therefore they are to be
inhabited as a place of ease rather than disease.

Tertullian is not the only Church Father to have preached
a doctrine of subjugation based on an unhealthy split or
division. A natural ordering of reality which sees man as
hunter and provider, woman as carer, is another of
feminism's targets. Not unreasonably women now realize that
a gender-based division of roles infantilizes female sexuality

and that this too attacks women in the body. It does this by assuming that female sexuality is the possession of those who 'own' the women in question. Namely their husbands or church leaders. Feminism can and must critique a social order which emphasizes productivity and promotes self-sacrifice as ultimate values, they argue. In the name of this ordering, too much violence has already been done to women. I have attended meetings where women argue about the vocabulary which should be used to describe this experience. I have heard advocates of 'intimate violence' lock horns with advocates of 'domestic violence'. But whichever way you look at it, the evidence is slowly and inexorably being assembled. And it is becoming clear that people who violate women's minds by treating them as possessions believe that they are allowed to act out this treatment in violent behaviour.

So it is not surprising that, once these connections are made, human sexuality and bodiliness become an arena for a political debate. No wonder that so much is invested in the question of ordination. After all, an ordained woman would, just by being there, actually demonstrate the perversity of the whole conspiracy. Nor is it surprising, therefore, that the 'family values' lobby are so vociferous in their opposition to this debate. In the name of a concern for 'traditional' values, they defend male dominance and female self-sacrifice without realizing that a serious discussion can only do good. This is because it would bring the insights of the gospels to bear in an area where extremists on both sides too readily claim the moral highground. At present the 'family values' lobby behave as though they are the only ones who value marriage and as though all feminists were violently opposed to it. This is hardly the case. Indeed the latest generation of young women academic theologians are keen to make the point that they value families – rather than 'family values' – and that they are anxious to explore new ways of parenting and providing for each other and their children.

So what are we to conclude about the very best of feminism? Firstly, that it condemns divisions or splits which make women suffer in the body. Secondly, that it sanctions a new set of role models for women. The more neurotic of the saints and the perfect wives and mothers have been replaced in the calendar of feminism by gospel characters. The bent woman of Luke 13.10–13, the widow who gives her money away in Mark 12.43, the crowd of anonymous, nameless women who surround Jesus; all are newly named by his ministry. I think of Phoebe the deacon of Romans 16, as well as the married couples Prisca and Aquila, Andronicus and Junia. I think of Thecla, the legendary disciple of Paul whose life was recorded in a second-century Acts of Paul. She was one of the first of the virgin saints and, until the fourth century, one of the most important women of early Christianity. Her life story is told in the Acts of Thecla which became immensely popular, so much so that bishops such as Ambrose quoted it frequently. She came from Iconium (modern Turkey) where Paul preached and she fell in love with him. She chose to drop an unsuitable fiancé and pledged herself to virginity, before taking off to follow Paul in his travels. Paul, meanwhile, ignored her and refused to baptize her. She baptized herself and, having fought off wild beasts and persecution, rediscovered Paul and told him she was now his equal. Paul had to agree and Thecla set off again to found new churches; the ruins of one of these still exist in Turkey.

All may stand upright as true daughters of God, defined in terms of their relationship to God, not along gender-based lines. At its best, this is the conclusion which feminism draws when it refuses to divide spirit from body or men from women on the basis of power and control.

There is a third insight as well, though. And this too is about the exercise of power. Only this time it is the planet which is the object of human control. Feminism has contributed to a new kind of ecological awareness. Just as women can no longer be defined as the possessions of men, so too the planet is more than the possession of human beings. Our relationship to it must be less exploitative, more caring and concerned. This means that a new metaphor for our relationship with the planet emerges which is enormously important for the debate about ordination. For women are now identified with creation in a new way.

This is powerful stuff, the plus side of which is clear to see.

For what we have here is an image of inter-connectedness and relationship and process and bonding. No wonder that feminist philosophy now argues that women's language and ways of relating to each other are about inclusion and synthesis. No wonder that the historians are coming through with the same message. It is evident that the contribution of women to the lives of our Churches has often been a corporate one. The religious orders, the Bright Hour and Sisterhood Groups, the great Guilds and Unions and Ladies Circles. All have worked well when they have been based on sharing and relationships and projects held in common. Indeed their contemporary counterparts, the most recent of women's groups, have chosen names which identify this very insight. So where the mid-nineteenth century could produce a group, founded to help cripples, called the 'Guild of Brave Poor Things', nowadays we have 'Websters' (named after the process of weaving) and the Methodist Women and the Catholic Women's 'Networks'. This insight is explored in language and imagery which focus on connections, integration, process and continuity. The harmony of relationships which feminism detects in nature is to be mirrored in the harmony of solidarity.

What about the negative side of feminism? What is the dark side of sisterhood and its hidden power? Firstly, I have a simple question, directed to the new understanding of the human body which feminism makes so attractive. Is there a subtle sense in which such a concentration on immanence denies women transcendence, in the name of rootedness to the earth? There are moments when all of us want to be more than what our bodies are being at and for and with us. Maybe a sense of transcendence is precisely what we need, and that too would go for all of us: women and men too. For the bent woman of the gospels is invited to stand upright, not simply to gaze at the earth. The widow becomes a model for people who want to make choices; her experience is not simply her own personal possession.

When working with a group of novices from a variety of religious congregations I set out some role-play exercises.

One took up this very theme. A religious community called the Ladies of the Glorious Ascension from Tunbridge Wells had run a prestigious girls' boarding school for many years. Recently some of their sisters had, however, moved out of this impressive environment to a seedy housing estate in which they were to be a presence alongside the poor. As it happens, one of their sisters was raped while returning home one night.

I asked the novices to assume the role of the Provincial Superior and her Council. As Ladies of the Glorious Ascension they had a responsibility. Would they tell the rest of the community about the event? What kind of aftercare would they offer the sister in question? What kind of theological resources would their charism enable them to bring to bear on the situation? In the feedback session at the end of their morning's work, they made an impressive presentation. Yes, they would tell the sisters. They were confident that these were adult, intelligent women who would not treat the sister in question as though she were untouchable. So far so good. All the positive insights of feminism – even though they did not use the word – were available to them and led to them to offer sound advice and counsel, notably about the care of the sister in question.

What they failed to do was to make the theological connection. They knew instinctively that the ascended Jesus took into heaven a wounded body, not a perfect one. So they could tap into the theology of human suffering which goes along with this understanding and accept that a sister who has been raped properly belongs in a religious community, as in any Christian community. But there is another one available as well to a woman who calls herself a Lady of the Glorious Ascension. She is more than the sum of what she experiences in the body. She is certainly not a victim; she has the capacity to be a survivor. In the language of my role-play exercise, I would argue that she can triumph in the body. Deliverance comes, though, when each of us realizes that we can triumph in the body and beyond the body because we are called into the fullness of participation in the Christian mysteries. Now saved, now risen, now glorified with Jesus. But the point is that we need this ultimate transcendence for the simple reason that the body does not last. Both its triumphs and its sufferings will end in the final decay of the grave.

So, too, with the second area in which feminism has offered women freedom. We are more than wives and mothers. And men are more than husbands and fathers. But who are our role models? What ordering of relationships is right when the natural order of subservience of women to men is abandoned? And what does this mean for women priests? How are they to exercise leadership if the only models which feminism values are essentially circular and egalitarian?

There is a further set of questions I want to ask at this point as well. And they must be answered as women are ordained. Those who speak eloquently about the inter-connectedness of women and nature have to be aware of the graces and of the hazards of what they are about. We need nature as never before. We are the first generation of human beings who know what the earth looks like from space, who can see how enchanting and precious and precarious it looks when viewed from beyond itself. We want the planet to survive. Indeed we can become quite sentimental about it. Yet, for all the beauty and fragility, I sometimes think that the planet is far more of a tough old nut than we imagine. And certainly capable of producing hazards and bacteria which will balance and defend its ecosystems more thoroughly than anything we can devise.

So what is the link with ordination? The lure of nature religion has always been strong and nature religion, of course, had a naïve theology of the inter-connectedness of women's bodies and the earth. Nature religion demands strange sacrifices. It offers rituals which celebrate a cycle of inexorable seasons, a haunting panoply of light and dark, life and death. It abnegates choice, because all is prefixed and determined, laid down in the dance of the spheres. All nature religion can do is dialogue with creation, as it were, to keep it going. No wonder that early Christianity set out new landmarks, honouring and respecting the cycles of light and dark, but juxtaposed to them, with liturgical seasons that do more than follow the inexorable spinning of the planet. The Christian year stands over and against the pagan year in the sense that its seasons acknowledge the changing seasons of the northern hemisphere, but they do more than this as well.

The Christian year is concerned to celebrate the birth, life and death of our Saviour. Its priests serve a God who leaps into life and the fullness of life, not one who is weighed down under the burden of the canopy of the stars. It would be a tragedy if feminism were to be side-tracked by a primitive understanding of science and cosmology – and women priests attached in the public imagination to something inexorably pre-Christian.

A more careful sense of the difference which Christianity actually makes would, it seems to me, enable women who aspire to ordination in the Catholic Church to do so without attracting the tag 'priestesses'. As with feminism, this is used as a derogatory label by the opposition. It is an ambiguous word because it sparks off primitive reactions. As priestessess serve a pagan god, they are not part of the new covenant which Jesus inaugurated.

How are women to aspire to ordination without attracting this set of associations? One route is the path of dogged asexualism, so that the person who is called to priesthood presents herself as dead from the neck down. I exaggerate, of course, but stereotypes, however much we must resist them, do convey the full extent of our pre-conceptions. So we have the cheery figure bending relentlessly over bike handlebars, off to save another soul. The austere one with her chilling bedside manner. The dedicated depressive; the manic narcissist.

Or there is the opposite route. The woman who is determined to offer the comfort of strange knowledge gleaned on the hillside after dark; the earthmother *par excellence*. Or the fey one, her eyes and crystals gleaming; the compulsive circle-dancer; the obsessive home-baker.

Somehow the question that feminism has raised will have to be met: namely, how can women inhabit their experience and their physicality with integrity and honour? All I notice here is that it has an additional edge when the idea of women priests is superimposed on some of the ideology. Are women to be feared because of the kind of prejudice a Maude Royden could identify as long ago as 1920?

Not even a beginning has been made in breaking down the peculiarly loathsome superstitions which bar the sanctuary to women. It is true that many people neither understand this prohibition nor are aware of its existence. It remains a fact that it crystallizes a prejudice indescribably insulting to womanhood, and one which, when a young woman first hears it, fills her with a very deep (and honourable) sense of resentment.[1]

This association of women and the sanctuary points up really sharply what some of the catches are. After all, what women seek is ordination in the one, holy, catholic and apostolic Church. Not in some sect. And that requires further work to be done reclaiming both our transcendence and our bodiliness. Then a third path will open up for women priests. One which accepts the beauty and dignity of woman's humanity in a celebratory style; one which seeks to build human community with all the building blocks God has given to us, and not simply with some of them; one which is realistic about nature and its limits.

Where can we turn to find a way forward? What can inspire some radical thinking? Feminism has enabled women to ask many of the right questions. What it now needs – in common with all theology – is to query its own presuppositions. Then it will inspire a new generation and continue to offer a valid critique. Which presupposition in particular should be re-examined if the logic of feminism is to be applied to the renewal of priestly ministry? Oddly enough, it is cosmology. Feminism has sometimes been naïvely associated with a wholly benign and romantic view of nature. In such a view technology is the enemy. The control that technology offers is a dangerous illusion. Rather than seek to control nature, we should submit to it. Indeed the violence of nature is even blamed on human interference – as though nature were not itself violent and destructive.

From science, though, come ways to understand both the predictable features of nature and the unpredictable ones. Chaos theory, for instance, is about the behaviour of irregular systems in nature. These are systems whose behaviour we cannot predict, but which combine stability with what are known as chaotic interludes. An example. The wind is blowing clothes on the washing line. In old-fashioned physics, if you knew the frequency of the gusts and the direction of the wind, its speed, the tension of the line and the weight of the washing, it was assumed that you would be able to predict the arc of the swing of each item of washing. Sheets would furl one way at one speed, socks another. But what physics now teaches is that these factors cannot be individually determined; the answer to your question about arcs and swings gets lost because you cannot determine the initial conditions with sufficient accuracy.

Anyone who has watched washing on the line in fact knows this already. It makes topsy-turvy patterns; it doesn't run like a car or a clock. No wonder a friend told me that, as a young married woman, she used to sing the metrical psalm 'I to the hills lift up mine eyes' as she hung out her washing. The balance of the words and tune would be matched by the random billows of sheets and wilful dance of socks. Nature is full of chaos. This is why it is so utterly fascinating and why we must never be simplistic about it. It is never either benign or malignant. These are human qualities that we project onto it. That is why we must lift our eyes to the hills. Not to confirm our identity with nature but to seek a way through and beyond it.

So as women priests begin to minister in the light of what feminism teaches the Churches, what are the blessings and what are the pitfalls? The blessings are obvious. We are invited to dismantle what I have called the conspiracy of control over women's bodies and sexuality. We are invited to search out new role models. We are to make connections and to explore our relationship with nature. In each of these ways, women who come to the altar have a glorious task. They are to be reconcilers as well as advocates and educators, confident that there is a theological underpinning for the work that lies ahead of them. This will be strengthened moreover, when they ask further questions of feminism. Like: What about transcendence? This is not simply to be dismissed as an act of the will, subjugating the body to its own control. What about the right ordering of human relationships? There is more to be said than is being admitted at present, because we have yet to discover a way of sharing human tasks that is not gender based and biologically determined. What about nature, and nature and women? Are we able to deal with the malevolent as well as the benign side of sisterhood – just as we have to reason with a destructive and creative side of nature?

So much for the logic of feminism as it examines the ways in which power and control have hitherto been exercised at the expense of women, rather than for the liberation of the human community. The next chapter must look at the methodology of feminism, what it looks like when it comes walking down your street and into your home.

NOTE

1 Maude Royden, 'The Lambeth Conference on "The Position of Women"', *The Guardian* (20 August 1990); quoted by S. Fletcher, *Maude Royden: A Life* (Oxford: Basil Blackwell, 1989), p. 198.

6

The methodology of feminism: storytelling, sisterhood and solidarity

When women are ordained and come to the altar, something new happens in all our Churches. Are ordained women to experience this new thing as a gift or as a burden? What about the rest of us? What expectations do we have of women priests? Feminism, by offering the bonding experience of shared storytelling, the political and social agenda of sisterhood, and by asserting the importance of solidarity in relationships, claims to offer a new way of meeting these expectations. Something new is offered to the whole Church – and to society as well – when women assume responsibilities which have been traditionally reserved for men. In this chapter I want to draw out what this means in practical terms. What does feminism offer? How can women work well – together, and alone? What are the snares? How can we avoid them?

Its methodology is simple. Feminism uses the simple process of sharing and storytelling to approach an important theological insight. It invites us to remember our story and to share the patterns which emerge as we reflect on the ways in which God has dealt with us. Then we can learn from these and grow more familiar with the ways in which God is likely to deal with us in the future. A method such as this obviously rates human experience very highly. It also values the capacity to catch this experience on the wing, and to become thoughtful and reflective about it. This is because it believes that, as we become more alive and sensitive to the workings of grace, so we become more responsive to the divine will. Call stories are an obvious example. Some are startling, like that of May Bounds, the Welsh missionary:

Then very suddenly I was shown what to do. I was off duty each Friday evening and had each Saturday free. I was spending the Friday evening at the Nurses Home called Scott House. I looked through advertisements of vacant posts for Nursing Sisters in the *Nursing Mirror*. There was one asking for Sisters to go to work in India where (at the time) there was only one trained Nurse for thousands of people. The longing returned to do Medical Missionary work. I knew again that evening it was the only thing I really wanted to do with my life.

The next morning I prepared to go to Chester on the bus and as I looked out from the window of my room I had what I can only describe as a 'Spiritual Experience'. In a split moment of time, suddenly away in the distant sky, there was a dark outline of India as on a map. Then instantaneously two strong arms came, embraced me and carried me strongly and swiftly to that India. Then with the sound of a click I was back into my shoes. In a fraction of a second I had been shown what to do.

I was dazed. This was broad daylight. I had no idea that such things ever happened. I went for the bus and to Chester for the day as I often did on my off-duty days. The one thing that stood out clearly was that I was directed to go to India. The experience was so humbling. I could scarcely think of what had happened without a feeling of emotion. Then I thought, when I tell my family what would their reaction be, but I wasn't ready to tell them yet and the spiritual experience was so personal and so very wonderful to me that I did not, or could not, speak of it.

Two days later I was again standing at my window thinking, 'well I am to go to India. I must make no mistake, I must go with the Church'. As I made this decision I was, as it were, filled to overflowing with a power that I have never before experienced. I had heard of the Holy Spirit and now I was myself experiencing it. I was filled with tremendous joy, difficult to describe. Such joy was coupled with deep humility. From then onwards I was able to tell people that I was applying to go to India as a Medical Missionary.[1]

This is an extraordinarily powerful account. Others are more prosaic because they result from a variety of encounters. A chance word, a book, involvement with an organization. But the consequences are as dramatic. It is not simply missionaries or nuns who tell these stories, they are part of the repertoire of any relationship with God. You could argue that Christian growth is all about fidelity to such calls: to hearing them and answering them with an increasingly loving and open heart. In working with Anglican women deacons over the past five years I have heard numbers of these stories. The focus is tighter, of course, because these women are hearing calls to priesthood. And now I am hearing such calls to priesthood from Roman Catholic women as well. They are related without apology and without fear; if anything they are told with a sense of wonder.

So what are they like? Many of the calls women have heard traditionally have offered personal holiness. They were calls to a way of life through religious consecration, for example. Now, while it is true that faithful nuns sanctify the whole Church, nevertheless outsiders have often seen theirs as a hidden way to God. This is a pity because it appears to privatize religious experience and make it the possession of an individual, rather than a gift to all God's people. Other women have received calls to a distinctive ministry of service, such as nursing or teaching: a named ministry with an identifiable clientele, lifestyle and structure. Characteristically the vocation of such women is also experienced as a gift which they receive from God and which will grow through the training they receive, the employment they seek and the results they then anticipate. Like the vocation of the nuns – and indeed, many of them are religious sisters – this is a personal experience, but the way it develops is somehow negotiated in the outer world. Theirs becomes less a private and more a personal call. Indeed May Bounds uses that very word. The invitation is more obviously there for other people to see and to experience as a gift to the Church.

But the calls women experience as God invites them to priesthood have a different feel to them. Here the vocation is not experienced as a private or personal gift. It comes from sources which are much more external to the individual who hears it. It does not promise holiness. It is not about a measured life of service. What it does instead is to expose women to the very fabric of God's dealings with the world. We are invited to stand at the place where God and the world are in conversation with each other and where women are needed both to pronounce judgement and then to be advocates of reconciliation and wholeness. The presence of women at the altar is an extraordinarily powerful sign of what it is that is done at that place.

No wonder a Church in which women are called to priesthood feels the stress and strain of their vocation so acutely. No wonder the Church is ravaged by it. After all, it represents a shift away from one whole world of meaning to another, and so it is extraordinarily costly to God's people.

By listening to stories like these ones about vocation, feminism teaches us that we may recognize history as a source of revelation. This should not surprise us of course. After all, the God of the Hebrew Scriptures, the God of divine revelation in Christ, is a God who is present to us, not absent from us. And this presence is not static. It cannot be so because God is revealed in the unfolding of human life.

But what is faithful listening? The Christian tradition has called it discernment and has been rigorous in searching out ways to do it well. Feminism too has the duty to listen faithfully because it is not somehow exempt from the disciplines of discernment we must all observe. Indeed, if – as is often said – women are good listeners, then we need these disciplines more than most people. Otherwise the experience of bonding becomes a tyranny. It is very easy to be swept into listening. Not all stories merit equal attention and it is hard to say 'no' when someone pours out a narrative where nothing is sifted, everything is assumed to be equally important. Yet discernment is essential for all of us to learn, especially for women priests who can mediate God's response. How are we – women or men – to listen well?

The most important of the disciplines of discernment is about setting up a further conversation. Raw human experience is not enough. If its secrets are to be unlocked, it has to dialogue with the Scriptures. In the world of Christian spirituality and retreat direction the consequences are evident. Women are empowering each other in the retreat houses as nowhere else because there we are listening to each other and offering encouragement to each other and validating a new reading of the gospel stories of Jesus. This is an enormously encouraging and moving experience.

Such storytelling is essentially egalitarian. My story can never be more important than yours. Both must be narrated. And both must enter into the dance of life which is only possible when they dialogue with the Gospel. Storytelling which fails to reach beyond itself to dialogue and dance in this way can be highly self-indulgent because it is uncritical. At its best, feminism is accutely aware of this; at its worst, it is not. So that we risk repeating over and over again the stories of our own oppression. And do so in a self-defeating way. An example. Much of the excellent work which has been done about women and violence in our Churches recently risks going down this route, because it claims victim rather than survivor status. Only this time this temptation is about communal rather than personal experience. And, for that reason, it is even harder to resist. In a group no one wants to be the unpopular figure who says 'enough'. There is a gospel perspective because all human suffering – of whatever provenance – can be gathered into the salvific mystery of the redemption brought by Jesus. I should not have to apologize for making this point, though I often feel I am being asked to do so.

What is to be negotiated here is some sense of balance. As with the immanence and transcendence debate, so too with the question of methodology. The human stories we have to tell are best fielded by a return to the stories of the Scriptures and to the transcendent Lord of these stories. Not by more and more – and increasingly uncritical – listening. And this is hard for women to negotiate when what we have always been told is that our great strength is our ability to relate to people, to get close to them, to do their laundry and cleaning and cooking, and now – on top of all that – to listen to their stories. All women who are actively engaged in ministry need to be aware of this. As a woman rabbi told a friend of mine: 'When people ask me to do anything for them, they say "Why aren't you? Why haven't you?" Whereas when they approach one of my male colleagues, they will say, "Would it be all right if? Would you please be able to?" '

So the method is about storytelling or faith-sharing. Its style is conversational. It invites friendship, even intimacy. And that is what is meant by bonding. But where the listening works well, it becomes something new, namely sisterhood. That is to say, it enables women to work collaboratively for change. This bonding together of women in common enterprises means that Christian feminists are led to take issue with a wealth of other concerns. So we turn to an analysis of psychology and sociology and come up with serious questions about what is proper and natural, what is well ordered and what is not. Where the nineteenth-century reformers rolled up their sleeves and tackled social reform in a hands-on style, we now have woman academic theologians who do the present-day equivalent. They campaign with all the vigour of their Victorian sisters but, in the light of twentieth-century science, are more articulate about what is proper or natural human behaviour, about what works well for women – and about what does not. So theory follows and is developed out of practice, but is informed by new knowledge. The good works of one generation are being translated into the good words and good practice of the next. But there is a bind. The Pankhursts, Emily Wilding Davison and the early campaigners who wanted the vote for women; Hannah More, Dorothea Beale and Frances Mary Buss who pioneered education for girls; Cecil Frances Alexander, Frances Ridley Havergal and the other women hymn writers who pioneered theological literacy for women: all of these were Christian women. They inhabited a Christian world.

Maybe they invited opposition but, by and large, it all came from one direction only. Namely from men – and other women – who opposed their challenge to what they understood to be a God-given Christian ordering of reality.

Whereas nowadays those academic women who take on the Church's teaching and submit it to scrutiny also take on the proponents of secular feminism. For secular feminism too is highly articulate about the place of women in society. Secular feminism trashes the Churches for what they have offered women; most Christians are terrified of secular feminists. And standing in the firing line are those women theologians who are brave enough to try to keep an open conversation going with both sides.

If we abandon or dismiss these women I believe that a double betrayal is being enacted. And what would be betrayed would be the roots of much Christian witness on behalf of women, particularly the contribution of the social purity movement at the end of the nineteenth century. Purity and social hygiene are not words which come tripping off our tongues nowadays. So what do they mean? Josephine Butler knew when she campaigned on behalf of prostitutes in British ports and barrack towns, to ensure that they should not be subjected to the humiliating demands of the Contagious Diseases Acts. Mrs Townsend knew when she started the Girls Friendly Society and gave young women the chance of a clean break from insalubrious homes and workplaces. Purity was not something which these girls had been born with and which they subsequently lost; purity is something which lies in God's gift and which we are offered every day of our lives. Not something women lose to men. It is these campaigners whom we betray when we abandon their late twentieth-century counterparts.

For the psychological and social agenda is timeless, however sharp its contemporary focus and however well informed by human sciences. So there is a challenge, and its thrust is two-fold. Feminism is right to remind us that the contribution of women to this conversation is essential; so that we should be subjects and not simply the objects of our moral destiny before God. But equally Christian feminism is left with a daunting task. Both to offer a critique of that church teaching which is constructed without listening to and consulting women, but equally to turn round to secular feminism and to say something sharp and contentious about the social issues of our day with the confidence that comes from knowing that, at root, Christianity is actually on the side of and not opposed to women.

Fertilization, contraception, euthanasia, care of the elderly, women in the workplace, the image of women in the media. All of these issues are now fiercely debated in contexts in which the Churches are completely discredited. That is why a decade of Churches in solidarity with women is timely. 'Whom shall I send?' says God to the prophet Isaiah. 'And who will go for us?' (Isaiah 6.8).

There are plenty of women who are hearing these words. And numbers of them answer, with Isaiah: 'Here I am Lord, send me!' And it is no longer good enough to say 'OK. So you can go as a church worker/pastoral associate/volunteer.' A radical shift is required if the witness of the ordained ministry is to make an authoritative impact in such circles. And once again the requirement is not about opting to be trendy or deciding to be a traditionalist. Nor is it simply about a blanket denial of the importance of the ordination of women. It is about drawing things both old and new out of the storehouse in the conviction that there is a Christian contribution which is weighty and honest and which works well for us all.

For this reason though, we should not be surprised that ours is an age that has produced both women theologians – including ordained priests and ministers – and men who are feminists. The evangelical task of proclaiming a saving word and of enacting reconciliation nowadays is daunting and God will surely call a new generation to meet this charge. Christianity claims to make a difference. Everyone wants to know what that difference looks and feels like; we want to talk about the issues which are at stake. A new and prophetic voice is being sought; but also we need a wise one.

Christian feminism wants to work for change by making a weighty contribution. Consequently it faces a further question. What happens when prophecy has to give way to wisdom? This is scriptural language and it conveys a dilemma which is all too well known to those who campaign for the kingdom. How can social and political thinking mature? How can we prevent it from deteriorating into the kind of politically correct mire in which ideologies lock horns and draw blood?

Where is wisdom to be found nowadays to match the strand of prophecy? One answer is offered by the idea of 'solidarity' which rightly emphasizes the human person and the importance of human relationships. Where does solidarity work and where can it not work? It worked very well in Poland in the 1980s. It does well when the context from which it draws energy and life is totalitarianism, and it can offer a valuable alternative. But once that totalitarian regime has been brought down, what do people really want next? On a visit to China in the footsteps of Gladys Aylward, Miss French and Miss Cable, and the other great women missionaries who had worked there, I saw this dilemma at first hand.

The word I heard most often was change. It carried many meanings. The first was to do with money and so was about exchange: for me this meant the ordeal of watching my passport pass through five pairs of hands as I tried to change a fifty-pound travellers' cheque at the bank. This is an economy as well as a workforce on the brink of a new revolution. That is why a prophetic voice works well in China, because it sanctions this quest for change.

Other evidence can be seen everywhere. And again the prevailing motif is that of exchange; for anyone with anything marketable sets up a stall. Enterprise is all. If you have got it, sell it. Clothes shops proliferate as the austere high-collared blue Mao jacket is replaced by an explosion of colour and style. Children in particular are dressed up to the nines. After all, where each family may only have one child (unless parents pay for the licence to have a second) the child has become a show piece. And of course most of these children are boys. The practice of infanticide which the missionary women knew all about is prevalent in China.

I photographed a woman in a white cap who was cooking sweet potatoes on the roadside and selling them to anyone who dared lift up the scorching skins in their fingers. She was furious with me for catching her unawares, ripped off her hat and ran her own fingers through her hair to strike a more flattering pose. But I had caught the image I wanted. An image of immense satisfaction and happiness and dignity. The pride of someone doing what she wanted to do. And making money into the bargain. Money which would open further doors and choices to her. I was led to reflect that, as oppressive regimes crumble, we have learnt that most people turn out to want something rather uncomplicated, like the freedom to experience their own individualism or a sense of self.

Now, feminism is not dealing with this when its prophetic strand continues to talk about solidarity and relationships, while women are asking for a new wisdom from it. More needs to be done to examine how the inclusivity represented by solidarity can be matched by the growth into personhood of the individual. How can feminism recognize individuals with their unique gifts from God? How can some women welcome the call to priesthood if there is a hidden agenda which is in fact saying 'either we all hear it, or none of us does'; or, 'unless you become a priest in the way I/we believe you should, you may not really be one'. How, in fact, can one person – whether woman or man – represent a whole group of people?

There are further questions as well. What about morality and ethics? Whose possession are they? Who writes the rules and why? And that, of course, raises the increasingly taboo subject of leadership. This must be addressed if only to put a stop to some of the naïve stereotyping which suggests that women excel at collaborating and enabling roles while men are best at having visions and exercising authority. This is a modern problem. It indicates how difficult democratic Christian people – let alone feminists – find it to choose, train and trust those who represent and lead them.

Each of these questions – about community, morality and leadership – must be examined if women are to be allowed to make the contribution to church life for which they are being called forward and ordained. Otherwise we will face a terrible irony as feminism could become the intractable enemy of priesthood some people already fear it to be. Only the priests this time would be the women. That is why the next three chapters must examine these three issues in detail.

In summary, then, the central insight of feminism is of extraordinary importance for the Churches. Namely that storytelling is a method and that it opens up a brand new dialogue with the Scriptures. The core value of social and theological engagement on behalf of women is rightly treasured by feminism. The centrality of relationships is rightly proclaimed by feminism. They do matter; they are at the heart of being human; they are the place where most of us meet God. In these three areas its methodology has been tried and tested and speaks with prophetic insight. What it must now do is distil a new wisdom with which to meet the sophisticated issues it has brought into being. And that means looking at what the Church is learning about community, morality and leadership.

NOTE

1   M. Bounds and G. M. Evans, *Medical Mission to Mizoram* (Chester: Handbridge, 1980), p. 8.

7

Making community

'Just as I am without one plea'; Charlotte Elliott's evangelical hymn sounds like an eclectic choice for a Roman Catholic nun to make in 1993 for a Select Preacher's Sermon in the University of Oxford. And so it was, in a way. Yet it was a choice which I made with complete confidence and certainty in May that year, as the sense of joy which had greeted the General Synod of the Church of England vote of November the previous year became edged about with anger and gloom. Individuals and whole congregations were beginning to come and go between the Churches, the newspapers told us. The more visible of these were, of course, persuasive in their denials of misogyny, eloquent in their defence of catholicity and the authority of the Roman Catholic Church. The less visible merely continued a trend which has been identified across the board, but which is a particular problem for the Roman Catholic Church: women in their forties who have successfully reared their children have suddenly had enough. Either consciously or unconsciously they stop going to church. And then they find they have left.

Some of these had already held the kind of attitudes Jeanne Pieper describes:

> Moderate feminists are a very large group within the Catholic church today, and more and more women are

joining their ranks. Their viewpoint is either 'What the Pope doesn't know won't hurt him' or they more or less consider the hierarchy of the Catholic church irrelevant to their own spiritual journey. Philosophically they are pragmatists. They use what they need and don't spend too much time and energy on the rest.[1]

The comment about spiritual journey is a telling one. As new ecumenical fault lines develop in the Christian imagination, as people begin to leave Churches, one area remains relatively unscarred. The world of spirituality. It can be criticized, of course, because it is subject to swings of fashion as the punters try out different prayer styles or brands of personality testing. It can be criticized because it leads people to privatize experience: 'my retreat', 'my prayer', and even 'my God'. It can be mocked because it produces gurus and groupies. But no one has yet had the nerve to say 'don't go on retreat', 'stop praying'. And they have never questioned that women cannot be good spiritual directors.

And so, as one set of fault lines opens up within the relationships Christians – let alone their Churches or ecumenical bodies – are supposed to enjoy with each other, how is it that the world of Christian spirituality is providing community for believers? What is it that they are getting right which the rest of us are somehow getting wrong?

When I chose Charlotte Elliott's hymn in Oxford, my theme was community, for the simple reason that the making of community now presents a challenge to the whole Church, not simply to any part of it such as the feminist movement, or the world of Anglo-Catholic loyalties, or the Roman Catholic Church. It is a shared problem, because the work of reconciliation is beholden on every Christian, not simply on a few enthusiasts. The question of community presses for attention in the wider political arena too, as well as in our own cities and neighbourhoods.

Later in that same year I visited the headquarters of NATO in Brussels for a briefing to church and other religious leaders. The purpose of NATO was obvious before the breakup of the former Soviet Union. It acted for the defence of Europe and North America. What about nowadays? The former Warsaw Pact countries have now become 'our co-operation partners' or 'partners for peace'. The Russian bear may have lost his threat. So at NATO, too, they are struggling with questions about community, about protecting the peace, maintaining stability and managing change. These are more than buzz words, these are the key constituent elements of what is seen as the way forward. For where peace, stability and change are well managed, the logic goes, then community will not suffer. And so it becomes possible to ask the bigger questions about who belongs. Who are the insiders, who the outsiders? How do we handle dissent? These are pressing questions and of deep concern well beyond our Churches. Only insofar as the Churches struggle to deal with them honestly as they experience them within and between themselves, will they be able to speak with any authority to a divided world.

Feminism claims to provide an example for building the human community by offering inclusivity and sisterhood; the Churches claim to provide an example by preaching tolerance. Both have been working with a model of unity which is presently being questioned by theologians and challenged by what is happening in Christian spirituality centres.

So Charlotte Elliott and her kind are not a red herring. Her spirituality complements my own. She brings book and word to bear on my sense of image and sacrament; she calls me to a conversion I never thought to undergo. Indeed, at the point where her church tradition and mine meet, I discover something characteristic of the private face of what I choose to call the new ecumenism. So where did I meet Charlotte Elliott and why did she seem important to me? I met her when I began to read outside the magic circle of Roman Catholic hymns and texts. I met her when I went to Evensong and began to worship with Christians from other Churches. I met her when I joined in a prayer group where people spoke freely about their faith and their favourite hymns and texts. And what I liked about her was that she was different from me, not the same as me.

I had sung Protestant hymns before ecumenism impinged on Roman Catholic consciousness, of course. It is just that they were attributed in the *Westminster Hymnal* of my childhood to an incredibly prolific author called 'Anon'. Anon wrote all the Wesleys' best hymns as well as those of Isaac Watts, Mrs Alexander and George Herbert, among others. Anon was a star of my youth. Sometimes I even imagined he or she was a real person. But all the time, a game of make-believe was being played. I was being asked to pretend that these authors were not different from me. For the duration of their hymn they were honorary Catholics, and then they could sink back into anonymity.

That is how the ecumenical world was configurated in 1956 when – to compound my ignorance – I attended a performance of the *Messiah* in Wells Cathedral in Somerset. Out came the Dean at half-time to lead us all in prayer. 'Our Father', he intoned, and I thudded to my knees. My brother hauled me back, hissing dramatically in my ear 'We don't pray with this lot'. Now this time something else was happening. I was being told that the Dean and the people worshipping in the Cathedral were different, but that different meant dangerous. And that I should preserve my own Catholicity by not mixing.

Times have changed. Thank God. In private, ecumenism now flourishes where once it was most publicly shunned, that is to say in inter-Church marriages. It flourishes where Christians from different Churches make friends with each other; where they share common interests and common causes; and, above all, where they find inspiration and spiritual nurture in the devotional practices and texts of each other's traditions. In private homes and in retreat houses in particular, the seams are hard to spot. Where concerns are shared, their inter-relatedness transcends sectarian divide. The weekend before I visited Oxford I had attended a meeting of the Irish Council of Churches Women's Link, an organization which also forms part of the hidden face of ecumenism, yet which brings together a group of more than eighty women with cross-border as well as cross-denominational concerns. Their theme was 'Lifestyle in the 1990s', as all-embracing really as Charlotte Elliott's about salvation and how we may appropriate it – and just as compelling. In each of these contexts, what is now becoming clear is that when you accept and love other people, you begin to value their uniqueness before God. And so a new model for community comes into being which will have far-reaching implications for those ordained to the ministry of proclamation and reconciliation we call priesthood.

In the meantime, as we struggle to understand what is happening before our very eyes, the public face of ecumenism is less of a seamless garment. And ecumenism's public face is, of course, considerably more familiar. Indeed it is excessively familiar to those who have been assaulted by the stream of newsprint about who joins or leaves whom because of the ordination of women. Onlookers could be forgiven for imagining that there were only two Churches in the United Kingdom. Forget the Free Churches, forget the established Church north of the border, and certainly forget the rest of the Anglican Communion. When push came to proverbial shove, Westminster and Canterbury appeared to be the only players. If anything it is for this reason that the very word ecumenical has been trivialized and cheapened, rather than because of anything God may have been doing in calling women in the Church of England – and beyond – to the priesthood.

It was not always so. At its best the movement for Christian unity over the past eighty years has led to an increased recognition, reverence and respect for each other on the part of the Churches. They have been trying to build community and have succeeded. People no longer want to be at religious loggerheads with each other. They are clear about the fact that they want to get on with each other. The question now is: how are we to do this? At its best, the ecumenical movement is in very good shape. In spite of what we read in the newspapers, the Churches are now closer than they have ever been. The myth that Christian unity was something which once existed and which has now been fractured is finally being exposed. Historical scholarship is showing us that primitive Christianity was extremely diverse, not the idealized pattern of the Acts of the Apostles.

What is happening, though, is a profound renewal of the theology of why and how we seek to make Christian community. Our theological template has changed and the new model enables us to face and, above all, to meet new issues and concerns.

In October 1989 I saw a job advertised in *The Tablet*. 'Associate Secretary for Women's Concerns', the copy ran, 'at the Council of Churches for Britain and Ireland.' As a concerned Christian woman and member of a religious community founded by Mary Ward, I thought I might have something to bring to the post, so I applied. After all, she had written in 1611 that 'women, in time to come, will do much'. And when she died just outside York in 1645, her sisters had discovered a vicar 'honest enough to be bribed' to bury her. Imagine my surprise therefore when, at the interview and when I subsequently began work, I discovered that the job had in fact changed its name and its identity. 'Associate Secretary for the Community of Women and Men in the Church' ran the brief. I had anticipated the women, was not antipathetic to the men, but to get community as well for good measure, let alone Church, meant that my hands were now full. Since then I have had regular opportunities to reflect upon the theology of community – and particularly its underlying gender implications – of many groups I have visited in England, Ireland, Scotland and Wales. I have been the guest of large institutions such as the Mothers' Union and Women's Guild of the Church of Scotland; I have eaten with small *ad hoc* groups in Greek tavernas and around kitchen tables; I have preached, exhorted, listened, laughed – and learnt.

What I now notice is that there is a theological understanding of community which has enjoyed enormous authority within the Christian tradition. This is the model of union with Christ. This certainly sustained me as I began to move out of the Catholic ghetto in which I was reared. It is easy to visualize it if you think of a sun with stars or planets around it. The person of Christ stands at the centre of the group: its centre, its sun, its very nub. Members of the group constellate around him. This image speaks compellingly to our desire to be united with him and his will for us. It answers

a deep need of the human heart and has provoked some of
the most lyrical of Christian writing and hymns. I am thinking
of Frances Ridley Havergal's 'In full and glad surrender / I
give myself to Thee, / Thine utterly and only / And evermore
to be', or 'Take my life and let it be / Consecrated, Lord to
Thee'.

This is the language of passion, desire and abandonment.
It is not surprising that writing such as this comes easily to the
pen of a woman. After all, the prevailing metaphor for union
in our culture is marriage. When Christians make
community, either wittingly or unwittingly, they often
attempt to replicate marriage, with a mother figure, a father
figure and little brothers and sisters. This is true even in
single-sex communities, such as religious brothers or sisters.
Members are encouraged into role and a certain immaturity
is expected, indeed encouraged, in those who are on
probation or junior members. Religious communities in the
Roman Catholic Church have had to do an immense amount
over the past 25 years to move out of a family model into one
which assumes that all members are adults and should both
act and, more importantly, be treated as such.

The marriage metaphor has other ramifications, though. In
church circles there are gender implications. Because men
look more like Jesus, they become the Christ icon in this
drama, and women, because they are different from him,
become the Church. At its most damaging this means that
men presume to tell women what to eat, to wear and what to
say. Also when they are to keep silence. The Church becomes
'she', Holy Mother Church, somehow identified with women
or the faithful, whilst men stand outside of this construct and
become church leaders. Or lay men, who will be consulted for
their professional skills but otherwise dumped, sometimes
sneered at behind their backs for not being quite spiritual
enough. That is to say, for not measuring up to an unspoken
requirement about celibacy.

A theology of union with Christ has other ramifications too.
Ones which affect groups and whole Churches as well as
individuals. Somehow an ideology begins to prevail where
some are declared to be more holy than others, that is to say,
more united with Christ. This has serious consequences for

the world of ecumenical relationships because it sanctions the mind set of those who, whether they are aware of it or not, are driven by a sort of spiritual snobbery. This leads members of a given communion or community to presume that they are closer to Christ than those who have fewer sacraments, for instance, or those who have no creed. Pedigree becomes all; the claims of antiquity reign unchallenged. The fullness of truth is assumed to lie in the past, where we once, supposedly, had it all together. Yet the study of early Christianity suggests that there never was 'one Church'. And Christ stands at the end of the age, at the pleroma, where true communion lies. We are all judged where convergence and uniformity are deemed to be the norm. Energy and youth get written off as that dreaded word 'enthusiasm'; enraged women are instantly labelled dissident or strident and dismissed; misogynists – men and women – can go church-hopping.

As an indication of how far the Churches have already come in their journeys together we need constantly to remind ourselves that we are more united now than we ever were in the past. The Bible is available and accessible to all in translations which have been agreed by a wide variety of church traditions. Eucharistic hospitality is possible where once it was always refused. The churches share moral concerns and act together on them.

The applicability of this model of union with Christ is evident if you are talking about Christianity. It is obvious that we want to be more like him, so we use language about growing closer to him. And growing closer means becoming more like each other as well as like him. Yet groups of like-minded individuals – campaigners for every cause and none – can only attract or repel. Belonging is all. And if you don't feel you can belong, then you must go. And if you don't feel that other categories of human beings belong – like women with vocations from God to the priesthood – then they must go.

This is a world in which priesthood is likely to be narrowly understood. The priest at the altar must represent Christ not only in action and ritual, but in gender too. And this suggests that he must be male. All the arguments which go the other way crumble before the rigour of this demand. So it is pointless to demonstrate that, if we are to take literalism seriously, then only 33-year-old Jewish men may adequately represent Christ. It is pointless to observe that the representation seems to be of Constantine as Emperor rather than of Jesus at Calvary. All that matters is the maleness of the priest. The maleness of Jesus is deemed to be more important than any other of his attributes. It becomes normative; everything else is to constellate around that fact. Either to be judged by it and found wanting, or to be affirmed and glorified by it.

There is, however, another model which is complementary to that of union with Christ. This is the model of community which is based on the life of the Blessed Trinity and it is becoming increasingly respected. It too has gender implications, it too generates a doctrine of representation which has serious consequences for priesthood. I would even say that it inspires all that is best in the new ecumenism; it is certainly known about in the world of Christian spirituality; it offers salvation to those who are struggling to deal honestly with dissent and reconciliation. According to this way of looking at things, the source of all our human aspirations for unity in Christ is the life of the very Godhead, the Blessed Trinity itself. We are to become more like God. This is our divine destiny. The picture changes completely; captured now by medieval stonemasons, now by Rublev's icon, now by the images of uncharted universes which dance the dance of space-time through our evolving universe, which we glimpse at from giant telescopes or from the tracks of tiny invisible particles.

When we consider this model of community, the tradition has always supplied us with a cast of three Divine Persons rather than two, so the marriage metaphor – powerful and useful though it may be – is no longer the norm. What we learn when we look at the life of the Blessed Trinity is that diversity is welcomed; what is important about each of the Divine Persons is their uniqueness. Yet together they are one God. Members of a Christian community who seek to represent the life of the Godhead are invited to explore a new asceticism. This is the asceticism of trust, mutuality and love because uniqueness is to be treasured; it is the very stuff of community.

What this kind of community requires of us is that we take the risk of being ourselves, even though this may mean being different from each other; it demands that we seek to understand each other by learning about and from each other. It proposes that God has in fact been at work both here – in what is known and familiar, but also there – in what is unknown and so less familiar – even in what is Anon or has been labelled Anon for the past four hundred or so years. It demands recognition, which means that we actually look at each other and learn about each other; it proposes that we stop persecuting each other for failing to live up to unspoken criteria about chromosomes; it asks us to love our enemies.

This new asceticism is especially appropriate in a world which is seeking to listen to the voices of women. Increasingly I find myself asking church leaders 'What structures are in place in your Church to enable women and men to listen to each other?' 'What training are you offering women, so that they can acquit themselves with dignity and style?' I believe these to be extraordinarily important questions. Because they alone will ensure that neither writes the scripts nor develops its rhetoric independently of the other. This work must be done in community.

No wonder that God is calling women to active public service in Church and society at this time. If the model of the life of the Godhead, in whose image and likeness women and men are made, is to work at all powerfully for us as we make this kind of community, then it has got to be seen to have the right ingredients. Representation matters terribly. A fragmented or partial picture cannot image God back to us. A representative priesthood must have women in its midst as well as men. For it is the work of God which is done at the altar; we do not come there to worship Jesus' maleness.

A further question. Is this not an even more pernicious constraint for women, making them yet more invisible, to choose a model of Christian community which has traditionally been described as Father, Son and Holy Spirit? I would argue that it is not. The trinitarian model has only excluded women when it has placed us outside the life of the

Godhead, as recipients of grace only, and never as its channels. I believe that we are at an important turning point in the Church's life. There is an altered perception nowadays of what it is to be a woman and this asks us to engage with a whole new range of questions.

One of these questions asks what God is like. After all, if women really are made in the Divine image and likeness, then we are talking about an altered perception of God as well as of women. Once again, we are, so far, only at the stage of attempting to ask the right questions. The answers have yet to be disclosed to us. For that reason I am inclined to offer caution to those who are busy trying to alter the gender of the Holy Spirit. As though the Spirit were suddenly to become 'right on' because we call it 'she'. That seems to me to be like moving the deckchairs on the *Titanic*. A far more radical restructuring will surely drive us back to the pages of the Scriptures where, hiding behind our preferred metaphors for God, a whole range of images wait to be reclaimed. In the name of these, Christian communities and Christian Churches will once again learn that women and men belong in virtue of their God-given humanity, not because of elaborate negotiations.

There are other objections to the trinitarian model. After all, hierarchy is discredited in today's world. And the Trinity is deeply hierarchical because the Father sends the Son, and the Father and Son in turn send the Spirit. Each of these actions is a procession which offers to one the role of sender and to another the role of sent. That is why Chapter 9 will have to investigate the idea of leadership.

More immediately, though, other questions follow from this discussion and analysis of community. These are about prayer and Christian living. About morality and ethics. When women come to the altar, what kind of instruction do they bring with them? It is questions such as these that I want to examine in the next chapter.

NOTE

1   Jeanne Pieper, *The Catholic Woman* (Los Angeles: Lowell House, 1993), p. 41.

8

In search of morality

In the introduction to this book I made two claims which touch directly upon the theme of this chapter. I hinted at a grave problem for all our Churches when I suggested that women are abandoning traditional teaching because it no longer speaks to their circumstances. I also suggested that the Catholicity of the Church is in question because its teaching and its sacramental authority no longer hold together. Let me look at each of these claims in turn.

Either in small groups or individually women are now discovering a sense of purpose and level of autonomy which mean that even the most devout will, on occasion, describe church teaching as 'high-handed' or 'irrelevant' by turns. At their most uninterested these women leave the Church or – as they would say – it leaves them. Where they are both interested and concerned and indeed loyal, they stay on. And as they do so, they read and study and discuss and pray with the Scriptures and find themselves making theology and examining ethics in a new way. This is the generation of women who are not afraid of excommunication, the Church's ultimate sanction. For years many of them have 'gone against' church teaching, because this is the group that was enfranchised – or disenfranchised, depending on how you look at it – by *Humanae Vitae*. These are the women who – either literally or metaphorically – take the pill.

When the history of the twentieth century comes to be written, its main achievements will be assessed. Already, though, people are anticipating the judgement of history and have their own private version of how we are to understand what has happened. The moon landings and birth-control would rate high on most lists, because they achieved something unimaginable to previous generations. Even nowadays it is hard to look at the moon and believe that human beings have walked on it. How much harder for our ancestors to imagine that people would actually travel into its icy-looking orbit, step down from their spacecraft and put human footprints on its dusty surface. So too with a world that was not distant and remote in the way that the moon is, but which was as mysterious. And which appeared to be governed by the same cycles and rhythms as the moon, namely the world of human fertility. Even nowadays it is hard to imagine what a revolution it represented for the secrets of procreation to be unlocked by science. How much harder for our grandmothers and great-grandmothers to believe that the control of their own fertility would ever be possible. My own great-grandmother had seventeen children, none of whom were twins, all of whom survived into adult life. In two generations we have spanned space and discovered the secrets of life.

If you were to ask which was the most significant of these two achievements, birth-control would win. To say that is not to take sides either to condone or to condemn. It is simply to state a bald fact.

What has to be noted, though, is that it is in this generation that God is calling women to priesthood. Not in the pre-pill era. Now it used to be thought that women were powerful because of the 'wise wound' of menstruation. Women alone could bleed and then, miraculously, stop bleeding. And blood, in primitive societies, is synonymous with life. The tacit understanding, then, has always been that women have control over life. This is not something which we have recently discovered. My great-grandmother with her seventeen grown children clearly had access to this power in abundance. What has changed is the way in which this control over life is exercised. Because of birth- or fertility-control, the knowledge somehow goes public. What was once known but unspoken is now writ large. A woman who can control the miracle, that is to say, choose when to bleed and when to stop bleeding, is doubly powerful. She exercises the most potent form of control known to humanity. No wonder that we hesitate to ordain her. No wonder that the Roman Catholic Church, by outlawing artificial birth-control and frowning on what is known as 'the contraceptive mentality', denies her the very right to existence.

But unless we make our new moral order with her – as opposed to without her – then her power will attack and punish us for our pride. Try as we may, we cannot restore a world which is ignorant of the scientific and technological advances of the twentieth century. It is in this world and not apart from it that the search for morality is on.

It is not simply women who have a problem here; we all do. So how are we to move forward? There is a sense in which a question such as this risks being totally abstract. So I want to demonstrate its importance by describing a very specific incident.

I was in Wales. The weekend I was attending was organized by a group of women who meet on an *ad hoc* basis every two years. They are called Benywdod a Duw, that is to say, Womanspirit Wales. I had been at their previous meeting as well and enjoyed the beauty of Gregynog, the University of Aberystwyth's extra-mural centre, as a conference facility. My own task was to address the group about the activities of the missionary women whom I had investigated for *The Hidden Journey*. I wanted to do something which would assess our confidence in the sources of salvation which had fed the missionary enterprise. Put simply, my question was 'Does the Gospel still work?' – with the rider 'And does it work for women?'

So I set up four role-plays. In the first of these, the residents of a small valley were invited to discuss the following question: 'The traditional industry of your valley is a high-quality paper mill, served by a stream. The paper is used to produce Welsh-language Bibles. The Welsh development board has decided to open the largest knicker-elastic factory in Europe there instead. Discuss.' I should add that the members of this group were all Welsh-language speakers, and discuss it they did, in an animated conversation where the only word I recognized was 'elastic'. They spotted the snare immediately. This was to juxtapose the merits of the Scriptures and female apparel. There were other, much wider considerations, such as the environmental question about the future of their little river. There was also the lure of big money which would mean jobs for everyone, and so a secure future for the community.

In the event they rejected easy compromise. No expandable scriptural quotes for them. They chose to resist the development board's plans. Instead they would become more pro-active; in future, they would seek to gain a voice in the production of the Bibles in question. The task of developing inclusive-language resources in Welsh is not an easy one. But these women were prepared to embrace it and give energy to it. They were confident that the Word of God is a saving word.

The second group had an equally daunting task. Their script ran like this: 'The United Kingdom has been taken over by the Thought Police. You are not allowed to meet, but choose to do so. One of your group has discovered a text hidden away in an old shoe box. She has brought it along to read it to the group. What do you decide to do with it?' This time they were English speakers. The text hidden in the shoe box was the Prologue from John's gospel: 'In the beginning was the Word.' As I chose it, I thought of the description of Dorothea Beale reading it aloud at Cheltenham Ladies College.

To Dorothea, to teach Scripture was an experience so deep and so wonderful that she longed to share it with every aspiring teacher. 'I should like most of you to look forward to Scripture teaching as a privilege to be desired', she told her staff. 'It is a sacred ministry, a sort of priesthood, this touching of sacred things, this breaking the bread of Divine knowledge for our children.' Her intense religious feelings could not fail to have an immense influence on the whole

College. 'I shall never forget the impression I received as a quite young girl', wrote one of her pupils, 'when I heard her read the first chapter of St John's Gospel. It was quite electric, one felt that this woman was reading the thing she considered the greatest in the world.' Even now, more than fifty years after Dorothea's death, those who heard her read St John's Gospel still speak of the experience as unforgettable.[1]

Dorothea Beale died in 1906. But the hair goes up on the back of my neck when I read that account of what the Scriptures – and the priestly task of breaking the bread of Divine knowledge – meant to her. I was disappointed in Wales therefore, in 1993, that this word no longer commanded such authority. The group in question experienced all the horror intended by the Thought Police scenario. If anything the role-play worked more effectively than I had anticipated. What they decided to do was to rewrite the text so that it would sound less toxic to any potential captors, and then they would destroy it by tearing it up and eating it. 'In the beginning was the artisan.' So much for the incarnate Word of God. So much too for the certainty that the saving Word of God can topple any system.

The third group, too, had a daunting scenario to deal with. I reproach myself with hindsight that I did not spell out the rubric quite accurately enough. For what was envisaged by my exercise was the experience of living in a Wales which had been declared a Muslim enclave, subject to the fiercest and most implacable kind of Shari'ah Law. A dispensation in which mutilation – for theft, for instance, as well as stoning to death for adultery – would be the norm. This was to be the unacceptable face of religious fundamentalism; not the warm and more familiar experience of Arab hospitality nor the friendly exchange of interfaith dialogue. The problem was that I did not make this clear. And so the group did not really grapple with the issue I had wanted to isolate. Namely the fact that there are norms which can be applied and that the Scriptures sanction this. The Bible helps us to identify and invites us to condemn violent, inhuman behaviour. We are never to walk by on the other side of the street. After all, what the missionary women discovered was that they had every right to condemn twin slaying, and the mutilation of footbinding, as well as temple prostitution and other practices which violated women. The Bible gave them this authority, as well as the authority to round on Christianity too when it was found wanting.

The final role-play took the case of a woman with motor neurone disease. This leaves the brain intact but incapacitates the body. Just as I had asked the other groups to consider, firstly, an ethical question about the environment and commercial pressures; secondly, an ethical question about the right to associate and to enjoy a personal, unmediated relationship with Jesus; thirdly, an ethical question about boundaries and limits and saying no to violence; so now I was probing an ethic of human suffering. What does a group of Christian women have to say to someone who is wasting away before their very eyes, yet who is able and indeed wants to talk about the process? They were desperately candid about the difficulty of speaking directly to the sick woman. How very much easier it is to organize reading sessions for her or set her up with meals than to risk an attempt to talk about suffering – even the suffering of Jesus.

None of these questions was about sexual ethics. I judged that ground to be too well trodden. In any case most of us regularly have to make decisions about how we use our money and our living space, our time and our spiritual resources, let alone our tolerance, our campaigning energy and our compassion to good effect. The examples may not be as extreme as those we grappled with in Wales, but the issues are just as pressing.

It is not simply Nicodemus who needs to come to Jesus by night. His wife too should be hammering at his door. But she is no longer doing so. That is how deep the disenchantment goes. I have said that I believe this is a problem for us all, not simply for women. The teaching ministry of the Church is failing to meet the spiritual aspirations of many highly sophisticated and intelligent women and men as well as those we rather patronizingly tend to call ordinary people or people at the grass roots. On this occasion I was the teacher and I failed totally because I had not realized how deep the chasm now lies. I am judged by this experience, but then so too are all who exercise teaching authority. What we are trying to say no longer makes sense.

Now I am not claiming that ministry will be renewed automatically by the ordination of women. But our teaching ministry clearly stands in need of renewal. In the exercises I had prepared in Wales, I was banking on the assumption that 'breaking the bread of Divine knowledge', that is to say, sharing the Scriptures, would automatically feed the sheep. This did not work. Even as a woman I could not make this happen for other women. Had I been an ordained woman, the same might have been true. This is not simply an issue about women ministering to other women. It is about how the Church which claims to minister to and teach women is constituted.

Where the root assumption is held that women may not represent Christ, that we may not stand *in persona Christi*, women are disowned and disempowered at the most profound level: the level of our very being. Many of the women who came to the meeting in Wales are Roman Catholics. Their sense of isolation and powerlessness affected us all. This is the inevitable consequence of the Church's present attitude to the ordination of women. We are separated from the sources of our sacramental system and from the authority or teaching structure which is inseparably bound up with it.

This is the further point about the teaching authority of the Church which I made at the end of the introduction to this book. By not ordaining women, I suggested, the Roman Catholic Church, in particular, risks separating its teaching and sacramental authority. I argued that this goes against the deepest instincts of Catholicism. And in Wales – and, let it be said, in many, many other parts of the world – I have seen what this means in practice. The simple truth of the matter is that women are teaching in both official and unofficial capacities; we have been doing so for years. When the nuns set up primary and secondary schools, when they opened their magnificent teacher training colleges, their intention was not to subvert the system. If anything, they had a conscious interest in upholding it. They upheld Catholic truth and were proud to teach it well. What has happened though is that the sisters, through much more immediate exposure to the pastoral reality of their pupils – the mess of abuse, drugs, loans to repay, sexual exploration – have begun to ask questions for which there are no pat answers. Their colleagues in the staffroom face the same dilemma.

Obedience once meant that Catholic teachers were simple vessels of communication who handed on the truths they had been taught. Fidelity meant doing this as well as possible. Every Catholic school the world over has graduation photos or year and house photos where the products of this enterprise are lined up for inspection. Fresh-faced, intelligent-looking children whose destiny it was to replicate the system. These are the boys who knew they could be priests, and girls who knew that they could not. Nowadays, though, the meaning of obedience has changed. It is a discipline which is beholden on us all and it means speaking as well as listening. After all, Mary's first words are not 'Let this be done unto me'. She asks a question, 'How can this be?'; she dialogues with the angel who comes carrying God's message, before she gives her consent. And she must be the model for our obedience.

So those who teach Catholic morals now have a new responsibility, to contribute to the discussion which is held where the eternal verities get formulated. Hence my point about the dangers of separating the teaching and sacramental authority of the Catholic order. How can the teaching and – increasingly – the preaching ministries of women be anchored or owned by the Church? This is not to say that you have to be ordained in order to teach. God forbid. What is needed though is a theological restructuring which admits that the authority which women bring to moral debate is now crucial. How is Catholicity to be restored if not by ordaining women?

Nature abhors a vacuum and especially a moral vacuum. And it is in the area of morality and Church teaching on right and wrong that this vacuum is beginning to yawn. The happy

divide that kept moral theologians off the backs of pastoral
practitioners, and which protected the ethicists from messy
pastoral reality, no longer quite works. Add the gender
question and you get a web of complexity.

This dissonance is experienced elsewhere too. Moral
teaching is desperately needed by society at large. We want to
be taught the difference between right and wrong, but
somehow have lost confidence in the ability of Church leaders
or of politicians to deliver such teaching. So we reach out for
people to blame. The media swing into the firing line, as the
easiest target. It is so easy to blame the press. Politicians and
royalty do this because they feel over-exposed to the public
eye; church people do this because they feel under-exposed.
They reckon their story never gets told and that it is only
scandalous stories of naughty vicars or perverted priests
which guarantee the kind of coverage for which they yearn.
But there is an ironic twist here. Because the media hold more
of a moral high ground than most other groups. After all, it is
they who point out the fallibility of our leaders, by running
stories which put their private lives up for moral scrutiny.

So then we try out other groups to blame for the ills of
society. Most recently in the United Kingdom, lone parents
have been singled out for attack, or people from racial and
ethnic minorities, or women who no longer work in the home.
In church circles we are inclined to blame 'lefty' clergy, or
fundamentalists, or women who are distracting the Churches
from their task of evangelization by all this talk of ordination.
And so the problem runs round in circles and does not get
addressed.

Where are we to find rest? Various options have been
adopted by church leaders. Firstly, there is the mindset which
produces documents such as Pope John Paul II's *Veritatis
Splendor*. This magnificent defence of the absolute centrality
of the human person is luminous and offensive by turns. It
sites the teaching authority of the Roman Catholic Church in
one place, namely the papacy, at the expense of other equally
important places, such as the local, that is to say, national
church. So that while, on the one hand, it reminds us that
morality matters and that morality is about people, not
abstractions; on the other, it sets up an impossible task for

itself, by being over self-referring in particulars. There is another moral mindset too, which abdicates any authority at all. So that anything goes or rather, because none of us in fact lives without rules, morality becomes the possession of an equally unself-critical coterie. What is the way forward?

In December 1993, the Roman Catholic diocese of Middlesbrough issued a statement on child sexual abuse. This provided information about the offender, the child and the issues raised for the diocesan faith community. As a priest of the diocese had been found guilty of paedophiliac charges and imprisoned for them, this was a live issue in this, as in many other diocese. A model of clarity and hence of good practice, the Middlesbrough statement had one section which stood out for me like a beacon. This is a 'Declaration of Children's Rights':

> God has given you the right to be cared for by people you can trust.
> God has given you the right not to be hurt in your body or mind by grown-ups.
> Never believe somebody who tells you a secret you must not tell your parents.
> Never believe somebody who says it is your fault that you are being hurt or frightened.
> God has given you the right to have your feelings taken seriously.
> If a grown-up does not take you seriously or believe you, you must talk to someone else.
> If you are uncertain about something a grown-up tells you to do, ask your parents or teachers about it.[2]

Any child would welcome such a clear endorsement of her or his rights. But, then, so would any woman. Substitute the word 'women' for 'children', substitute the word 'men' for 'grown-ups', and you have a text which the Churches have yet to write. Christians do have rights of course, it is just that men seem to have more of them and more substantial ones than women.

It follows that all our morality is skewed to service the needs of men over and above those of women. It follows that women are objects rather than moral subjects. It follows that women can only ever be the passive recipients of sacramental grace and never, with Christ, its initiators. I could go on. But, as I argued in Chapter 3, there is no point formulating these rights when our theology of the proper role and dignity of women is equally skewed because it is determined by our biological function. Only by ordaining women, that is to say, by publicly overturning a theological order which says that biology is destiny, will justice be done to women.

The Middlesbrough experience is worth reflecting on. A core group of nine clergy and lay people, including a teacher, clinical psychologist and forensic expert – all of whom are women – produced the nineteen-page diocesan statement. Here we have an *ad hoc* team assembled to meet a distinct pastoral need; here we have professional women and men working alongside their priests and bishop. Here we have an indication of how things might be done. In the secular domain the women in question enjoyed representative status, that is to say, they could carry the needs of the human family on behalf of us all. Even the Church knew that.

In the secular domain they could be leaders. And briefly, for once, they could be that for the Church as well. Had they done this at a time in which women were ordained as priests in the Catholic Church, something additional would have been done as well. The sacramental thrust of what they were doing would also have been available in representational form for God's people. Their role *in persona Christi* would have been identifiable too because it would be celebrated at God's altar as well as in the diocesan boardroom.

NOTES

1   J. Kamm, *How Different From Us: A Biography of Miss Buss and Miss Beale* (London: The Bodley Head, 1958), pp. 243–4.
2   *Diocesan Statement on Child Sex Abuse* (Diocese of Middlesbrough, 1993), p. 17.

9

Leadership and the ordination of women

Nancy Kennelly is pastoral associate at a brand new church outside Chicago. There are 3,500 families in the parish with 2,000 children following the religious education programme. This goes up to eighth grade, that is to say girls and boys who are fourteen years old when they leave. The parish priest is sixty-two years old. The archdiocese faces financial chaos. Change is the order of the day. At St Elizabeth Seton's, meanwhile, Nancy Kennelly's ministry is thriving.

Nancy is an IBVM sister, like myself. I visited her at the school which served as a temporary home for her congregation in 1989 and in Chicago itself in 1993. She has held a leadership role of some eminence within the Institute of the Blessed Virgin Mary, serving as Vicar General or second-in-command to the General Superior for a number of years. During that period she also worked with the state penitentiary, doing one-to-one work with prisoners. Nancy is old enough to carry the legacy of pre-Vatican II Catholic piety. This gives her a range of sacramental know-how which she can apply in the most testing of circumstances. 'I know I bring the feminine side of the Church in pastoring to these people', she says of her work at St Elizabeth Seton's. When I asked what that meant she gave me a string of examples. She blesses the tombstone of a lost baby with holy water and a prayer; she carries a Host to the parents of a child who is to be taken off a life-support machine, touches the baby's body with it and then shares it with the parents; she has prayers for miscarriages, for people whose first time back to church is to attend a funeral, for those who seek the healing of a failed marriage. As a field advocate for the diocese, she takes testimonies from women and men who need an annulment of their first marriage. This she sees as a healing process of immense importance, offering, as it does, the chance for reflection and the possibility of preparing for a new marriage. She is never permitted to preach, though she may give the homily at a eucharistic service. A eucharistic service is a form of the Mass which omits the consecration of the bread and wine; communion is administered from the reserved sacrament in the tabernacle.

When she broke her shoulder in a car accident, she had been carrying holy water in the passenger seat. As she was borne away to the ambulance, strapped down to a stretcher, she insisted on taking the holy water bowl and hyssop with her. Next day was Sunday and they would be needed at her beloved St Elizabeth Seton's! One consequence of this devotion is recorded in an aside she made to me. 'People say to me that they prefer Sister's Mass to Father's Mass.' She is now reluctant to offer the people the opportunity of going to eucharistic services. However great the pastoral need for them, essentially they enable the archdiocese to avoid the issue of the ordination of women.

Brenda Egan, meanwhile, is a younger sister. She is one of a chaplaincy team of fourteen at Loyola University in Chicago. When I met with her she described the team and her work. It has been set up over an extended period of twenty years by a lay woman, in response to the needs of the student body at Loyola, one of the finest Jesuit Universities in the United States. For this reason it has been possible to ensure a good balance of five lay people, five religious sisters and four priests. Brenda herself gives retreats, hears confessions and presides in different ways at student liturgical celebrations.

She is indifferent to what she describes as 'the white feminist movement which pushes for equality and ordination'. She is more concerned with womanist theology because it advocates visibility for black women like herself. 'You could clericalize women', she said to me with a shrewd look on her face. 'I have no call to join this boys' club.' What she insisted on, though, was the need for training for leadership, authority and pastoral care.

When I contrasted my experience of these two visits I realized that leadership was the common thread between them. Here are women who are occupying leadership roles of considerable importance. What difference would priesthood make to them? Is the ordination question a total red herring? The Church after all is *semper reformanda*, but does the perpetual cycle of renewal necessarily include the ordination of women?

After all, the traditional way has worked very well and here are two women who, in common with many others, are working alongside and collaboratively with the present system, just as it stands. Why bother to introduce change?

The present system is based on two theological presuppositions. One has a scriptural basis; it says that Jesus chose women to be disciples and men to be apostles. The other has its basis in the symbolic ordering of reality: it says that the Father sends the Son into the world and so it establishes a male chain of command. Both of these are about leadership and the exercise of authority because, inexorably at present, in the Catholic system, you cannot exercise the fullness of any leadership role unless you are male and you are ordained. Only the ordained may lead. Until some women are ordained as priests, all women and all lay men are deprived of any true leadership identity within the community. Only with the ordination of women will it become possible for the laity to assume the fullness of their calling to leadership because, at present, in spite of the wonderful work which is being done by many of them, leadership and priesthood have become interchangeable words. That is why I want to look at each of the theological presuppositions in turn as a way of

examining their basis in reality, as well as a way of advancing
a new insight into Christian leadership.

The disciples/apostles conundrum neatly mirrors the
argument about women as carers and men as providers. It is
the spiritual equivalent and perpetuates the same biologically
determined myth. This time, of course, what women are
invited to provide in their caring role is incredibly attractive
because it asks the very best of us. We are to follow Jesus by
ministering to the needs of his people. Now 'needs' is a code
word, some people say. What it actually means is that women
are allowed to do all the invisible and unglamorous bits of
church life. And that they will be sanctified thereby. Men,
meanwhile, are to be apostles. That is to say, they are to go
into the world and tell people that Jesus is risen from the
dead. Theirs is the public, proclamatory role. After all, they
were first called by Jesus, sent out in twos by Jesus and then
they were there at the Last Supper. And we all know where
the women were. In the kitchen. Except for Mary. Perhaps
she was in some oratory, lost in contemplation, not dragging
a dishcloth around greasy mutton stains.

Three things need to be said at this point. Firstly, that to
be an apostle is to be a witness of the resurrection. The
fullness of any Christian call can only be determined in the
light of the resurrection. This, after all, proclaimed a new
reality, an endtime in which all is made new. Now, clearly,
Mary Magdalen was the first of the friends of Jesus who heard
a command to go and tell the good news of his resurrection.
And whom was she to tell this to? How were they identified?
Not as apostles – after all, she was that – but as brethren.
Secondly, it was not men whom Jesus chose at the Last
Supper to represent him. It was bread and wine. He did not
turn, now to Peter, now to Judas and say of them 'This is my
body'. He took bread instead. And thirdly, the fact that eating
arrangements in first-century Palestine may or may not have
meant that women and men sat down to eat together is a
distraction. Nowadays we do sit down to eat together. How
well is our eucharistic theology informed by this reality?

The Last Supper is of course crucial, but not as an exercise in barring some and admitting others to the altar. The Last Supper is crucial because it offers us four actions which set out the true meaning of the apostolic call. When we concentrate on the bread and the wine, instead of the people who may or may not have eaten it, we see what this meal offers the Christian community.

If we are to be a Christian community – as opposed to rather an un-Christian one – then 'Alleluia is our name', in Pope John Paul II's memorable words. We are indeed a resurrection people, but also we are a Last Supper people. We are a community which is taken, blessed, broken and given, just as our Saviour was.

Each of these words repays reflection. For not only are we are a community which is taken, blessed, broken and given, but as individuals too – whether we are priests or not – this will be the pattern of our personal lives when they are conformed to the life of Christ. No wonder it is so important for us to listen to call stories like those of May Bounds and the other missionary women. No wonder it is so important for us to listen to the stories of present-day women who tell us that God is taking them by choosing them for ordination. When we look at the totality of the pattern of God's dealings with women, we see how the vocations of the former have prepared the way for the vocations of the latter. Not simply in the missionary field, but as well on the 'home front' women such as Elizabeth Fry, the friend of prisoners, and Edith Picton-Turberville, the social and political campaigner, have prepared a way for the Lord and the Lord's new call to the Church.

There is more to reflect on, though. For taking means separation as well as election. For centuries we have concentrated on what the ordained are separated from. The defence of such disciplines as celibacy has devoured our energy. Whereas it might be even more useful, just at present, when the reception of married Anglican clergy into communion with the Catholic Church is undermining public confidence in the absolute need for celibacy, to ask a different question. This would be less concerned with purity and the separation of a celibate caste from, say, women, for instance. Instead it would ask what separation is for. What are the tasks

of a priest? And what, distinctively, are the tasks of the laity?
How can we construct these according to the charisms which
God gives to people rather than along gender lines? The
whole Church will benefit when we begin to address these
questions because in this way, all our relationships will be
renewed.

And what about the God who chooses people for
leadership, including priesthood? What do we learn about
God when we begin to explore our own eucharistic identity?
God is disclosed to us as a God of desires, the 'passionate
God' whom Rosemary Haughton wrote about so
compellingly, as long ago as 1981. Because God does call
people and in this act of calling is revealed to us as a yearning
God. We all have defences for dealing with the God of desires,
and none works greater damage than sheer deafness.

Yet words like 'conformed to the life of Christ' are emotive
and quite hard to hear; the language of desire is highly
charged. It speaks to our deepest desires as well as those of
God. In the name of religious desire, many women have been
swept along a path of self-surrender and sacrifice which has
destroyed them. This is because Christian asceticism too
readily forgets the second of Jesus' eucharistic gestures. Both
as a community of believers and as individuals we are blessed
by God. Only when we have been visited by the God of
blessings can we safely take our place at the foot of the cross.
Historically, many more women have been broken than have
been blessed; the blessing of ordination is a timely one. This
is because the altar, too, is a place of blessing and women are
needed there to offer as well as to receive this blessing.

Once the sense of election and of blessedness have taken
root in the eucharistic community and individual, then it is
safe to face the self-gift which is intrinsic to our service of the
Gospel. God does not want damage to be inflicted on people
in the name of love. But true love is self-sacrificing because it
is about making choices, and some of these will always be
made at personal cost to ourselves. In the name of the God
of costly love we take up the daily burden of being open to
costly choices. In this way we too will be broken, but broken
as bread is broken, in order to be shared.

And in the sharing, too, both as individuals and as a group, the Christian community most truly finds its eucharistic and apostolic identity. Because when we share the good news of the passion, death and resurrection of Jesus with other people, then we round off the meaning of what we do at the altar. Without proclamation, our experience of salvation remains a private possession; with proclamation – when we assume the fullness of our eucharistic identity – it becomes a gift to others. Now, if this is true for the worshipping community as a whole as well as for individual believers, then clearly what it means for all of us is held in trust in some special sense by those who exercise the charism of leadership. This makes it clear that this charism cannot be founded in gender differences. Men and women cannot have different eucharistic identities. For we are 'one bread, one body' and united too in the one apostolic call to share the news of our redemption.

The apostolic call is a call to leadership because it is a call to witness that we have been taken, blessed, broken and given. Our eucharistic identity has taken root in us; we too may take, bless, break and give in our turn. It is God who calls and marks those who are to witness as priests and those who are to witness as lay people. We cannot tell God whom to call and what to do. But we can value leadership given by ordained women and men just as much as we do by lay men and women, and we need to learn to start doing so.

Having said this, I notice a further phenomenon. When do people learn that they have a vocation to the priesthood? Very often this happens on retreat. Amongst the means of grace given to the Churches to help us discern priestly vocations are the *Spiritual Exercises* of St Ignatius of Loyola. In retreat houses all over the world, women and men go on retreat and give each other these spiritual or prayer exercises. They are a powerful means of identifying and training priests. The optimum experience is to make the retreat over a four-week period in seclusion and silence. Each day is interrupted only by an interview with the retreat director, who suggests texts for prayer for the following day. These will be taken from the *Spiritual Exercises* themselves or from the Scriptures.

Ignatius' text follows a very well-ordered plan. During the first week, the individual retreatant is invited to consider the fact that as a world and as individuals, we stand in need of redemption. God's healing is addressed to human need; what does this need look like in the world around me and when I consider my own history? The high point of this week comes when I realize that the work of my redemption has been done. I experience this as an enormous release of energy and joy which empower me to turn to the second week of the retreat. Here the focus changes. My prayer is now centred on the mysteries of the life and ministry of Jesus. I hear him calling his apostles, and calling me. I watch him healing the sick, and healing me. I hear him teaching the crowds, and teaching me. I move with him towards the experience of the third week which opens, tellingly, with the Last Supper. Then I move slowly through the events of Passiontide and go with him to the sufferings of Calvary. In the final week of the retreat, Ignatius invites me to wait upon the risen Christ and experience the cosmic significance of his conquest of death.

Now, as I have described it here, this sounds like a gender-free experience. But in many cases it is not. A subtle kind of screening goes on. There are certain retreat directors who, knowingly or not, have so internalized the idea that women may only be disciples and men apostles that they in fact inhibit the course of the retreat. Typically, they keep women retreatants in what I choose to call 'first-week mode'. So great is the emphasis they place on the healing of painful memories that they withhold the retreatant from any sense of release, of energy and of joy. It is perfectly possible to spend four weeks in retreat without ever getting into the material which Ignatius really wanted to have examined in weeks two, three and four. This, if you like, is because no one speaks openly about the politicization of the retreat experience. Politicization is an ugly word, but it is an ugly practice too because, in effect, it ensures that women do not hear the apostolic call of week two, the priestly call of week three, the evangelical call of week four. Instead they limp through the text, constantly tied to a set of unspoken perceptions. It cannot be by chance that the entry point of week three is the Last Supper. It cannot be by chance that many women retreatants barely make it to that point.

When I first wrote about this in an article in the *Supplement* to *The Way* in 1991, I deliberately chose to use the stories of a couple of imaginary retreatants to demonstrate my point. In this way I intended to make a measured introduction to the idea that, as retreat directors, we are not as free as we sometimes think we are. The irony now is that I realize that those who go on retreat may also be colluding with the same idea. If women do not believe they can hear apostolic or priestly calls, then they will not hear them. So much for grasping the nettle that will enable us to identify not simply priests, but a whole gifted gathering of individuals who may exercise leadership roles in our midst.

I have indicated, too, that there is another question to be faced if any discussion of Christian leadership is to provide fresh information, and not simply churn out past certainties. This is about the symbolic ordering of reality. In the Catholic tradition revelation is understood to be a hierarchical process. It goes from the Father to Christ and thence to the world. All truth comes from above and is disclosed to us from on high. This is an enormously consoling doctrine to those for whom it is familiar. The very Catholicity of the Church is seen somehow to stand or fall on this ordering because it is a unique model with a variety of applications. It is used by the Church as a whole and by individual parts of it too. So many dioceses and parishes are run like this as well. Everything logically comes from the Father to Christ and then to the one who stands in the place of Christ, at the altar, at the lectern, at the Christening party, the parish jumble sale, the annual financial audit and so on.

If there is a problem with this model, it is simply that it anticipates a male line of procession. While the gift of God's life and grace in Christ is destined for the world, the tradition has sent it to us via a male mediator. Some extraordinarily passionate, indeed sexual, imagery has been used to describe how the process works. One theologian from the Orthodox tradition used language that suggests that priesthood involves impregnating the world: 'The man as witness acts by his virility, with his priestly energies he penetrates the flesh of this world, he is the "violent one" of whom the Gospel says that he takes possession of the kingdom by force.'[1] This discredits the whole notion of divine procession which is intended to be about the self-gift and self-disclosure of God.

This is why it is worth looking at the experience of the women's religious orders. For here an older tradition of celibacy is observed where the procession of one person of the Blessed Trinity to another to the world is configured differently. Many of these large religious communities are run by and for women. This introduces an interesting precedent. Not only can women offer each other the witness or apostolic identity of leadership but also we can stand *in persona Christi*. At the end of the chain of self-gift and disclosure, a woman too can be called to mediate grace and reconciliation and call these forth from others. I turn to Ignatius of Loyola again for a textual reference. In the *Constitutions* which he wrote for the Society of Jesus, but which are used by many women in what is loosely called the Ignatian family, we read: 'To make progress, it is very expedient and highly necessary that all should devote themselves to complete obedience, by recognizing the superior, whoever he is as being in the place of Christ our Lord, and by maintaining interior reverence and love for him.'[2]

The women's orders have changed the pronouns but retained the insight. No wonder Mary Ward and her first sisters, along with many of the great women who founded the old-established women's congregations, were aware that they were bringing 'some new thing' to the Church. Not only did they want their sisters to make the *Spiritual Exercises* – and so to hear the call to an apostolic and priestly life – but they also wanted a spirituality for mission which would defend the right of a woman general superior to hear God's call and act upon it. In 1615 Mary Ward wrote 'And it will be seen, in time to come, that women will do much'. We have to contemplate the idea that, in prophetic and free spirits such as her, the seeds of women's vocations to the priesthood first saw the light of day because she and the other founders laid the tracks for women to exercise the roles and functions of leadership.

But there is more to be said. For not only can and do women stand *in persona Christi* in their own religious congregations, but also – both in these congregations and well beyond them – other authority structures are being developed and with them new images of power and authority and leadership and control which can and should inform our priestly practice.

Now, what is envisaged by such developments as these is not a watering down of truth. That would be to destroy the understanding that God uses human means to sanctify the world. What is envisaged by these developments is not a leaderless Church. That would deny the gift of leadership which God so clearly gives to some, and not to others. What is envisaged is not some murky kind of pluralism, so that anything goes. Instead what is being explored by such groups is something profoundly Catholic, namely a consideration of the fact that the Word of God was conceived in a woman's body and brought forth from her to save us all. I say that this is a profoundly Catholic notion. Yet, as I suggested in the introduction to this book, the lines are blurred. No wonder that Thomas Torrance, theologian of the Reform, can write so compellingly:

We conclude that in spite of long-held ecclesiastical convention, there are no intrinsic theological reasons why women should not be ordained to the Holy Ministry of Word and Sacrament: rather, there are genuine theological reasons why they may be ordained and consecrated to the service of the Gospel. The idea that only a man, or a male, can represent Christ or be an *ikon* of Christ at the Eucharist, conflicts with basic elements in the doctrines of:

the incarnation and the new order of creation,
the virgin birth, which sets aside male sovereignty and
    judges it as sinful,
the hypostatic union of divine and human nature in the
    one Person of Jesus Christ who is of the same
    uncreated genderless Being as God the Father and
    God the Holy Spirit,
the redemptive and healing assumption of complete
    human nature in Christ and the atoning sacrifice of

Christ which he has offered once for all on our behalf, in our place, in our stead.

And therefore it conflicts also with the essential nature of the Holy Eucharist and communion in the body and blood of Christ given to us by him.[3]

NOTES

1   Paul Evdokimov, *La Femme et le salut du monde* (Paris, 1979), pp. 210–11; quoted by Elisabeth Behr-Sigel, 'The ordination of women', *Theology*, XCVII, 775 (London: SPCK, 1994), p. 14.
2   St Ignatius of Loyola, *The Constitutions of the Society of Jesus*, tr. George E. Gauss SJ (St Louis: Institute of Jesuit Sources, 1970).
3   T. F. Torrance, *The Ministry of Women* (Edinburgh: The Handsel Press, 1992), pp. 12–13.

10

Crowned with the sun

In the Catholic tradition, at the place of encounter and reconciliation where God and humanity meet, there stands a woman, Mary the mother of Jesus. John Paul II's encyclical letter *Mulieris Dignitatem* teaches that 'The sending of this Son, one in substance with the Father, as a man "born of woman", constitutes the culmative and definitive point of God's self-revelation to humanity. This self-revelation is salvific in character.'[1] *Mulieris Dignitatem* also reminds us that the Council Fathers of Ephesus were the first to accord extraordinary dignity to Mary. It was in 431 CE that she was first proclaimed to be the mother of God. They used powerful language because the situation was extreme. The incarnation meant that the divine nature of Jesus was born as well as the human nature. Now how could this truth best be defended? The Council Fathers decided that the answer lay in asserting that Mary was the mother not simply of Jesus in his humanity, but of the eternal Word in his divinity as well. She was declared *Theotokos*, or mother of God.

So who is this woman and how are we to understand her and what she may be for us nowadays? There is no more powerful ally to any Roman Catholic than the Virgin Mary. For this reason she has her champions in every theological nook, cranny and bywater in the Church; preached now by some as a model of submission and femininity, now by others as a warrior for freedom. This latter role may come as a surprise to some, but Mary the friend of the poor is an ally of the oppressed in many Latin American countries as well as in the nations of the former Communist bloc. The former role is, of course, much more familiar because it has been used in art and iconography as well as in church teaching.

It has to be said, however, that to those outside the Catholic fold she presents a twofold problem. Her cult is perceived to be an obstacle to the proper worship of her Son because she appears to detract due attention from the person of Jesus. Or there is another group – and this has happened more recently – for whom she is a bone of contention. Certain feminists see only the externals and are enraged that her cult should be based on a circular argument: the Virgin Mother being an impossible role model for any woman to follow as well as a dangerous fantasy, they would say, to hold up before men. To be an advocate of the Virgin Mary and to try to explore what traditional teaching about her may disclose in our own times is a difficult and dangerous path to steer therefore. For she belongs to all of us and yet to none of us, because the truth about her will only be revealed to us in the fullness of time. Nevertheless, any attempt to explore the place of women in the Church must take account of her. It cannot be conducted in isolation from her, for hers is an image of great power, able now to attract and now to repel. This discussion is about power and authority and leadership and control. For that reason, if for no other, it is worth examining how a Catholic view of Mary can inform the debate about women and their ordination.

In particular, what has she to offer the Church as we seek to understand its symbolic ordering of reality? I want to turn again to a Catholic text to examine how this reality is constructed. In his *Spiritual Exercises*, Ignatius of Loyola gives us a variety of theological insights about the place of Mary. In the very first week, he proposes a meditation which employs the three powers of the soul, namely memory, understanding and will. This is a meditation on the place of sin, and our memory of sin. Ignatius directs us first of all to contemplate Christ our Lord by imagining what he calls the material place where the Exercise is set. Then he says 'I said the material place, for example, the temple or the mountain where Jesus or his mother is'. So, right at the beginning of the *Exercises* Ignatius demonstrates that for the purposes of prayer and meditation there is a choice of visual representation. That somehow the fullness of the divine image is offered to us by a contemplation of the faith life of Mary, just as it is by looking at the faith life, or saving ministry, of Jesus. She has the mind of Christ and so can represent the mind of Christ.

This suggests that there are other choices to be made in our understanding of reality. One is about our imaginative starting point. Ignatius calls it 'the material place', and gives examples such as the temple or the mountain. He could equally have said the altar. The point being that each of these is, as it were, morally neutral. Each serves as a trigger as we begin to interpret and apply symbolic meaning to the material place. The Catholic tradition relies heavily upon this separate layer or interpreted level of meaning, particularly in its sacramental system, insofar as its sacramental system requires outward signs but assures inward grace. If there is discussion and debate in the Catholic world, therefore, it happens at the second level, that of the interpretation of meaning, rather than that of the original and material starting point. That is why many Catholics are mystified with the preoccupations of some of those who seek admission to their Church as women are ordained elsewhere. For they detect a kind of absolutism in their quest which ill accords with the Church's sense of eternal value and ultimate meaning, and with the sense of spiritual detachment which is a prerequisite to genuine conversion. The Catholic Church is, after all, a teaching Church and this requires from all who belong to it a significant degree of openness. Catholicism in general, and Ignatian spirituality in particular, have a name for this attitude of spiritual detachment: it is called indifference. This is a grace which Ignatius has retreatants pray and pray to receive, so central is it to the discernment of Christian choices. That, I believe, is one reason why he sees that we need to understand the mechanisms we use to create meaning. It certainly explains why Ignatius illuminates these so clearly in the *Exercises*.

In the third exercise of the first week, for instance, he gives another key text which shows one of these mechanisms at work. This is a description of what he understands by colloquies or prayers of encounter and petition. Here he attributes even more importance to Mary because he inserts her within the symbolic representation of the Blessed Trinity: 'The first colloquy will be with our Blessed Lady, that she may obtain grace for me from her Son and Lord for three favours.' Secondly, we are to turn to her Son – for Jesus is identified by his relationship to her, rather than with a simple 'then turn to Jesus', or 'turn to the Divine Majesty'. And finally 'I will make the same requests of the Father, that he himself, the eternal Lord, may grant them to me'. Here a trinity is placed before us. Another trinity which consists of a female representation, her Son and the eternal Father.

In the dynamic and purposes of the *Exercises* Mary is made available to us to do the work of the Spirit in our lives. She is the one whom we can turn to in order to ask for graces from her Son and Lord. She mediates the grace of Christ to us. Mary is placed with her Son just as the Son is placed with the Father and we too can turn to her and find our own place.

Here we have the theological key to Catholic Marian devotional piety. Here we also have the key to modern discomfort with devotional piety. For there are many people who feel profound disquiet as they read an analysis such as this. On the one hand, as I have indicated, the pure strand of Protestantism discounts any cult of the mother because it distracts from the Son. Indeed, at its most extreme, the iconography of Protestantism has no female figures at all. It is not simply in our cathedrals that these have been destroyed. Women have been written out of the statuary and art and hymnody which would represent the human in chapel and church; let alone whatever might represent the divine. And lest this be seen as a legacy borne simply by the Churches of the Reform, it is worth noting that these attitudes are now current in the Catholic community as well. For on the other hand, contemporary Catholic liberalism is embarrassed by popular devotion to Mary as well as by traditional teaching about her. After all, devotional piety is inclined to be for the unlettered. You do not have to be able to read to say the Rosary. Anyone can memorize the Litany of Loretto. Late-twentieth-century Catholics are reluctant to associate themselves with devotional practices which pre-date Vatican II. The irony is that Christians of both the Reformed and Catholic traditions – as well as the well-informed agnostics who are called on to chat shows to mull over these issues: artists, painters, writers – are all equally ill at ease with Marian devotion.

I want to examine the consequences of these attitudes insofar as they affect our understanding of the ordination of women to the priesthood, for the simple reason that one reason why the cult of Mary attracts such hostility is that it is about honouring a woman; it requires us to concede that a woman has power and authority within God's plan; and that she may make choices which indicate a level of autonomy and control over her destiny. So that when we examine why the cult of Mary is suppressed by various interest groups in all our Churches – or encouraged by others which have a distinct political agenda – we have a clue, I believe, to understanding why much of Christian theology (of whatever kind) has a deep investment in institutionalizing misogyny.

It is easy to understand the antipathy of Protestantism; after all, it has an inner coherence and logic as part of a distinct and definite protest. Its misogyny is a product of certain scriptural and theological choices, though much has been done recently to redress the balance. It is easy to understand the reluctant hostility of present-day biblically literate Catholics; this too is logical insofar as it also seeks to find a new balance and sense of direction. If it is misogynist, this is by default. In their day-to-day devotional life, many of the faithful have been deprived of sacramentals which were highly user-friendly to women. These have yet to be replaced. I can also understand why feminists are squeamish; Mary has indeed been used to abuse the religious sense of Christian women. No wonder, I should add, that certain right-wing groups within the Church claim to colonize some sort of moral Marian highground. They want her to remain docile, to occupy the niche in her Lady altar, to cradle her child. In her they see a model of subservience which keeps a whole social order intact. One which means that a dominant or ruling class is paid for and lives off the generosity of the few.

The irony is that both these groups are of necessity bound together, because their arguments are determined by the fact that Mary bore Jesus in the flesh. No wonder they are doomed to persecute each other.

So here we have a gallery of vested interests which collude in preventing Mary from climbing down from her plinth, because each – in a subtle way – has gone down the avenue identified by Edwin Muir in his poem 'The Incarnate One'. For Muir, writing here about Calvinism, identified the fact that we do strange things with the Christian mysteries. The person of Jesus and the salvific events of the life of Jesus are read and reread in every time and season. You do not have to have a very well-developed sense of history to see what this might mean.

Muir himself saw the 'logical hook / On which the Mystery is impaled and bent / Into an ideological argument' as a simple transition: 'The Word made flesh is here made word again.'[2] While words can clarify and explain, they can also obscure and conceal. When the Word becomes flesh, God is made present and explained to us in the person of Jesus; when we persist in making him Word again, it is as though, in our own attempts to clarify what it can mean to say that God is with us, we seek to remove the mystery of the incarnation. Instead we try to make it somehow terribly safe, an idea which can inhabit our minds without touching our bodies. In this way, Muir suggests, we persist in impaling and bending the incarnation into something which it was not, by talking ourselves out of believing in the fact that the Word was made flesh.

After the incarnate Lord, Mary is the second casualty. For hers was the flesh Jesus first took, blessed, broke and gave. If we had stayed with this mystery, we might have seen a range of meanings which would not have been available otherwise. For when the Most High overshadowed her, Mary did more than conceive Jesus: she assumed the power and dignity given to all who are obedient to the will of God. By removing this understanding from our theology, we displace Mary – and all women with her. In their place, we put a deeply secular model, based on biological determinism of a most primitive sort.

The destiny of women proclaimed by the incarnation of

Jesus in the flesh of Mary is a destiny which uses the natural order but is not constrained by it. I have identified four areas in which I believe it to be essential for us to understand what this means for priesthood and for Christian living: they are related to power, authority, leadership and control. Mary's power comes from her authority not simply as the mother of Jesus in the flesh, for she is more than that. She is the mother of God. For Jesus was born 'not of male will' (John 1.13) but of God. Now it is not surprising that we react to the idea that a woman is invested with so much authority. It is not surprising that the biblical narrative of the annunciation story and Catholic teaching about the Virgin birth are challenged today as never previously. After all, they challenge all the norms on which our society is constructed. They upset all the secular models which Christianity was intended to transform, notably the understanding that biology is destiny. This masks as an ancient and spiritual tradition, but is not. If biology were destiny, Mary would be no more than the mother of Jesus in the flesh. But instead she is more than that; her identity in the symbolic ordering of things means that she can stand before and with God. Notice the fact that I am not saying that she has the power to be autonomous in herself. This autonomy is always defined in relationship and obedience to God. She has a distinctive place in the dispensation of grace because of her relationship with God.

So what have Christians done with the Church's teaching about Mary as mother of God? In the name of a return to the text, to the authentic experience of the first Christian community recorded for us in the books of the New Testament, the Protestant tradition strips her of this dignity. It is dismissed as a later excrescence, added by the Council Fathers at Ephesus, it is argued. The Catholic tradition too turns the tables on Mary. In the place of the Christbearing mother of God, we are offered a stripped-down version, the anodyne Mary who is our mother but somehow disallowed as mother of God. Indeed in 1964, when Paul VI declared her to be mother of the Church, this shift was formally incorporated into Catholic teaching.

But devotional piety cannot so easily be 'made word again'.

In the spiritual lives of illiterate people, such as the women and children who have been visited by visions of Mary, or the powerless and weak casualties of totalitarian regimes, she remains the strong advocate who is friend of the poor and means of grace. The mediating, priestly role of Mary is kept alive in such communities, often to the embarrassment of their clergy. Her power and authority survive there intact.

The apparitions have been recorded on some twenty thousand occasions in the past seventy years. Women and children have seen her in countries as far apart as the Ukraine – where she appeared in black on the anniversary of Chernobyl – and northern Japan. In Cairo she has been spotted on the roof of a mosque by Muslim garage mechanics. In Ireland her statues dance and move in the sun. Most tellingly of all perhaps, the visions at Medjugorje in the former Yugoslavia have called people to contrition and repentance. Is this mainstream Catholicism, or a shadow, folk side which must be rooted out and destroyed?

Is it surprising that Marian devotion is so strong in Poland, where the strong image of Our Lady of Czestochowa has been an inspiration for solidarity and struggle? But equally is it surprising that, with the downfall of the totalitarian regime there, the image and the cult have been reclaimed from the people by their clergy, so that they now become an organ for communicating a surprisingly traditional doctrine of the human person, otherwise known as man?

Meaning is never straightforward. It is constructed in some surprising circumstances. Rosemary Radford Ruether has described a visit to the community of Tres Personas Solo Dios in the Philippines, where an understanding of Mary's role in popular piety has been taken to its logical conclusion. The community lives on Mount Banshaw, 'a sacred mountain for many Filipinos. It is still a largely untouched region with dense forests and clear, natural streams. Several churches developed in these mountains from Catholic and indigenous roots about 100 years ago, dedicated to preserving the natural environment against exploitative development and also to a mystical vision of the liberation of the Philippine islands from foreign colonization.'

Sometime in the 1960s, this community decided to have only women as priests, based on their view that males were not able to remain celibate . . . There are seven women priests who reside in the community house next to the church, along with a number of women servites who are in preparation for the priesthood. The women priests who are called padre, celebrate a Mass on the holy days, which fall on the seventh, 17th and 27th day of the month.

The women priests wear sky blue with a white cape and a kind of bishop's hat. In both this church and the Cuidad Mystica, Mariological imagery is related to a vision of the messianic woman and the New Jerusalem of coming redemption to the islands.

These communities seem to express, in indigenous and folk Catholic terms, many of the concerns that are constitutive of a liberating vision: leadership roles of women alongside those of men, communitarian socialism, defense of ecology and liberation of the land from neocolonial domination.[3]

In a word, what we have here is an example of a folk tradition which has found both a practical and a theological solution to the question of priesthood *within* its Catholic heritage, as opposed to apart from it. And Mary supplies both the theological hook and the imagery for the needs of this community. An extreme example certainly, but nonetheless interesting for that. For here the power and authority of Mary are assumed by women in a totally unself-conscious way. They then take on priestly roles in the community and begin to exercise the control that go with their authority.

So that this particular folk tradition accepts the power of Mary and the power of all women with a singular degree of sophistication. This power is not mediated through an earth-mother figure, a cosmic goddess for whom body is all. Neither is it mediated through the sexual coupling of the priest with the Church or with a human partner; it is not biologically determined. Woman is more than the sum of her female organs. So the women priests of Tres Personas Solo Dios observe a discipline of celibacy.

It is a nice irony that this insight comes to us with all the

eloquence of the voice of the poor. The trouble is that we are
not particularly good at listening to the voice of the poor, in
spite of our protestations to the contrary. And, in any case, it
is easy to dismiss antics in the Philippines as an aberration
from the truth.

It seems to me that the best corrective both to the mystery-
breakers identified by Edwin Muir and to the mystery-makers
visited by Rosemary Radford Ruether is to look once again at
the mysteries themselves and how we mediate them. When
Mary assumes her rightful place in the symbolic ordering of
reality, we too may take ours. Whether we are women or men.

What does this mean for the exercise of priesthood in our
Churches? Our priests are ordained by God to celebrate the
sacred mysteries of our redemption. Their power comes from
their obedience to God; their authority from their
relationship to God; their leadership comes from God and is
to be exercised in the spirit in which it is given.

The first time I attended Mass celebrated by another
woman was in a dream. I was in an underground chapel,
waiting with a congregation of students and their teachers for
the priest to show up. He was not there – whether delayed or
absconding I do not know. The congregation grew uneasy;
how would our need be met? It was at that moment that a
sister from my own congregation appeared, crowned with the
sun. That is to say that she moved forward in a stiff dalmatic
from the sacristy, adorned with precious stones and stiff
brocade. She came foward hesitantly, radiantly, reverently
and celebrated the Mass with total concentration and
prayerfulness. I looked at her carefully when she first emerged
from the sacristy and with a degree of shock. For in reality this
sister is deeply wounded. After a lifetime of faithful and
invisible service, she now has Alzheimer's disease.

Why did my psyche choose her as celebrant? I wonder; and
with that question, I return to what I said at the beginning of
this book. Women are now moving from the invisibility and
obscurity of centuries of hidden service. The glory of Christ
can be revealed in them in ways that have hitherto been
unimaginable because our imaginations have been withheld
from contemplating the Theotokos, the mother of God
revealed as mediator of grace. So that nowadays, when we

speak about offering God service at the altar and celebrating the mysteries of a fully inclusive redemption of all humanity at that place, we must not be surprised that God is calling women to offer that service and to celebrate those mysteries.

NOTES

1 John Paul II, *Mulieris Dignitatem* (London: Catholic Truth Society, 1988).
2 Edwin Muir, 'The Incarnate One' in *The Penguin Book of Religious Verse*, intro. and ed. R. S. Thomas (Harmondsworth, Middx: Penguin, 1963), p. 55.
3 Rosemary Radford Ruether, 'Not only are women priests; only women can be priests', *National Catholic Reporter* (4 September 1992), p. 14.

The following organizations campaign world-wide for the ordination of women in the Roman Catholic Church.

Australia Women of the New Covenant, 18 Second Avenue, Brunswick, Victoria 3056, Australia.

Eire Brothers and Sisters in Christ (BASIC), The Presbytery, Saint Francis Willow Vale, Avoca Avenue, Ballybrack, Blackrock, Co. Dublin, Eire.

Korea Korean Catholic Women's Community, 11-2 Ch'ung Moo Ro, 2ka, Chung-ku Seoul, Korea.

The Netherlands Foundation Vrouwmens, Sophicweg 133, 6564 AB Nijmegen, The Netherlands.

United Kingdom Catholic Women's Ordination, c/o Myra Poole, 7 Harwood Terrace, London SW6 2AF, UK.
St Joan's Alliance, c/o 36 Court Lane, London SE21 7DR, UK.

United States of America Women's Ordination Conference, (Membership) PO Box 2693, Fairfax, VA 22031-0693, USA.

Appendix

Ordinatio Sacerdotalis

ON RESERVING PRIESTLY ORDINATION TO MEN ALONE

Apostolic Letter of His Holiness Pope John Paul II

Venerable Brothers in the Episcopate,

1. Priestly ordination, which hands on the office entrusted by Christ to his Apostles of teaching, sanctifying and governing the faithful, has in the Catholic Church from the beginning always been reserved to men alone. This tradition has also been faithfully maintained by the Oriental Churches.

   When the question of the ordination of women arose in the Anglican Communion, Pope Paul VI, out of fidelity to his office of safeguarding the Apostolic Tradition, and also with a view to removing a new obstacle placed in the way of Christian unity, reminded Anglicans of the position of the Catholic Church: 'She holds that it is not admissible to ordain women to the priesthood, for very fundamental reasons. These reasons include: the example recorded in the Sacred Scriptures of Christ choosing his Apostles only from among men; the constant practice of the Church, which has imitated Christ in choosing only men; and her living teaching authority which has consistently held that the exclusion of women from the priesthood is in accordance with God's plan for his Church.'[1]

   But since the question had also become the subject of debate among theologians and in certain Catholic circles, Paul VI directed the Congregation for the Doctrine of the

Faith to set forth and expound the teaching of the Church on this matter. This was done through the Declaration *Inter Insigniores*, which the Supreme Pontiff approved and ordered to be published.[2]

2. The Declaration recalls and explains the fundamental reasons for this teaching, reasons expounded by Paul VI, and concludes that the Church 'does not consider herself authorized to admit women to priestly ordination'.[3] To these fundamental reasons the document adds other theological reasons which illustrate the appropriateness of the divine provision, and it also shows clearly that Christ's way of acting did not proceed from sociological or cultural motives peculiar to his time. As Paul VI later explained: 'The real reason is that, in giving the Church her fundamental constitution, her theological anthropology – thereafter always followed by the Church's Tradition – Christ established things in this way.'[4]

In the Apostolic Letter *Mulieris Dignitatem*, I myself wrote in this regard: 'In calling only men as his Apostles, Christ acted in a completely free and sovereign manner. In doing so, he exercised the same freedom with which, in all his behaviour, he emphasized the dignity and the vocation of women, without conforming to the prevailing customs and to the traditions sanctioned by the legislation of the time.'[5]

In fact, the Gospels and the Acts of the Apostles attest that this call was made in accordance with God's eternal plan: Christ chose those whom he willed (cf. Mk 3:13-14; Jn 6:70), and he did so in union with the Father, 'through the Holy Spirit' (Acts 1:2), after having spent the night in prayer (cf. Lk 6:12). Therefore, in granting admission to the ministerial priesthood,[6] the Church has always acknowledged as a perennial norm her Lord's way of acting in choosing the twelve men whom he made the foundation of his Church (cf. Rev 21:14). These men did not in fact receive only a function which could thereafter be exercised by any member of the Church; rather they were specifically and intimately associated in the mission of the Incarnate Work himself (cf. Mt 10:1, 7-8; 28:16-20; Mk 3:13-16; 16:14-15). The Apostles did the same when they chose fellow workers[7] who would succeed them in their ministry.[8] Also included in this choice were those who, throughout the time of the Church, would carry on the Apostles' mission of representing Christ the Lord and Redeemer.[9]

3. Furthermore, the fact that the Blessed Virgin Mary, Mother of God and Mother of the Church, received neither the mission proper to the Apostles nor the ministerial priesthood clearly shows that the non-admission of women to priestly ordination cannot mean that women are of lesser dignity, nor can it be construed as discrimination against them. Rather, it is to be seen as the faithful observance of a plan to be ascribed to the wisdom of the Lord of the universe.

The presence and the role of women in the life and mission of the Church, although not linked to the ministerial priesthood, remain absolutely necessary and irreplaceable. As the Declaration *Inter Insigniores* points out, 'the Church desires that Christian women should become fully aware of the greatness of their mission: today their role is of capital importance both for the renewal and humanization of society and for the rediscovery by believers of the true face of the Church'.[10] The New Testament and the whole history of the Church give ample evidence of the presence in the Church of women, true disciples, witnesses to Christ in the family and in society, as well as in total consecration to the service of God and of the Gospel. 'By defending the dignity of women and their vocation, the Church has shown honour and gratitude for those women who – faithful to the Gospel – have shared in every age in the apostolic mission of the whole People of God. They are the holy martyrs, virgins, and the mothers of families, who bravely bore witness to their faith and tradition by bringing up their children in the spirit of the Gospel.'[11]

Moreover, it is to the holiness of the faithful that the hierarchical structure of the Church is totally ordered. For this reason, the declaration *Inter Insigniores* recalls: 'the only better gift, which can and must be desired, is love (cf. 1 Cor 12 and 13). The greatest in the Kingdom of Heaven are not the ministers but the saints.'[12]

4. Although the teaching that priestly ordination is to be reserved to men alone has been preserved by the constant and

universal Tradition of the Church and firmly taught by the Magisterium in its more recent documents, at the present time in some places it is nonetheless considered still open to debate, or the Church's judgment that women are not to be admitted to ordination is considered to have a merely disciplinary force.

Wherefore, in order that all doubt may be removed regarding a matter of great importance, a matter which pertains to the Church's divine constitution itself, in virtue of my ministry of confirming the brethren (cf. Lk 22:32) I declare that the Church has no authority whatsoever to confer priestly ordination on women and that this judgment is to be definitively held by all the Church's faithful.

Invoking and abundance of divine assistance upon you, venerable Brothers, and upon all the faithful, I impart my Apostolic Blessing.

From the Vatican, on 22 May, the Solemnity of Pentecost, in the year 1994, the sixteenth of my Pontificate.

(John Paul II)

NOTES

1 Paul VI, *Response to the Letter of His Grace the Most Reverend Dr F. D. Coggan, Archbishop of Canterbury, concerning the Ordination of Women to the Priesthood* (30 November 1975): *AAS* 68 (1976), 599.
2 Cf. Congregation for the Doctrine of the Faith, Declaration *Inter Insigniores* on the Question of the Admission of Women to the Ministerial Priesthood (15 October 1976): *AAS* 69 (1977), 98–116.
3 *Ibid.*, 100.
4 Paul VI, *Address on the Role of Women in the Plan of Salvation* (30 January 1977): *Insegnamenti*, XV (1977), 111. Cf. also John Paul II, Apostolic Exhortation *Christifideles Laici* (30 December 1988), 51: *AAS* 81 (1989), 393–521; *Catechism of the Catholic Church*, no. 1577.
5 Apostolic Letter *Mulieris Dignitatem* (15 August 1988), 26: *AAS* 80 (1988), 1715.
6 Cf. Dogmatic Constitution *Lumen Gentium*, 28; Decree *Presbyterorum Ordinis*, 2b.
7 Cf. 1 Tim 3:1-13; 2 Tim 1:6; Tit 1:5-9.
8 Cf. *Catechism of the Catholic Church*, no. 1577.
9 Cf. Dogmatic Constitution on the Church *Lumen Gentium*, 20, 21.
10 Congregation for the Doctrine of the Faith, Declaration *Inter Insigniores*, 6: *AAS* 69 (1977), 115–116.
11 Apostolic Letter *Mulieris Dignitatem*, 27: *AAS* 80 (1988), 1719.
12 Congregation for the Doctrine of the Faith, Declaration of the Faith, Declaration *Inter Insigniores*, 6: *AAS* 69 (1977), 115.

Bibliography

William M. Abbott (ed.), *The Documents of Vatican II* (New York: Guild Press/London: Geoffrey Chapman, 1966).

Cecilia M. Ady, *The Role of Women in the Church* (London: Church House Publishing, 1948).

Bonnie S. Anderson and Judith P. Zinsser, *A History of their Own* (London: Penguin, 1988).

Gillian Avery, *The Best Type of Girl* (London: André Deutsch, 1991).

Hatty Baker, *Women in the Ministry* (London: C. W. Daniel, 1911).

E. Moberley Bell, *Storming the Citadel: The Rise of the Woman Doctor* (London: Constable & Co. Ltd, 1953).

Kathleen Bliss, *The Service and Status of Women in the Churches* (London: SCM Press, 1952).

Kathleen Bliss, *The Future Of Religion* (London: C. A. Watts & Co. Ltd, 1969).

Bramwell Booth, *Echoes and Memories* (St Albans: The Campfield Press, 1925).

Evangeline Booth, *Woman* (New York: Fleming H. Revell, 1930).

May Bounds and Gladys M. Evans, *Medical Mission to Mizoram* (Chester: Handbridge, 1980).

Lavinia Byrne, *The Hidden Tradition* (London: SPCK, 1991).

Lavinia Byrne, *The Hidden Journey* (London: SPCK, 1993).

Diocesan Statement on Child Sex Abuse (Diocese of Middlesbrough, 1993).

Lina Eckenstein, *Women under Monasticism* (Cambridge: Cambridge University Press, 1896).

Lina Eckenstein, *The Women of Early Christianity* (London: The Faith Press Ltd, 1935).

Jacqueline Field-Bibb, *Women towards Priesthood* (Cambridge: Cambridge University Press, 1991).

Austin Flannery (ed.), *Vatican II: More Postconciliar Documents*, vol. II (New York: Costello Publishing Company, Inc., 1982).

Sheila Fletcher, *Maude Royden: A Life* (Oxford: Basil Blackwell, 1989).

Roger Fulford, *Votes for Women* (London: Faber & Faber, 1958).

General Synod Debate (November 1992), *Ordination of Women to the Priesthood* (London: Church House Publishing, 1992).

Jane Grierson, *Isabella Gilmore, Sister to William Morris* (London: SPCK, 1962).

Hansard, Parliamentary Debates, House of Lords Official Report, vol. 549, no. 194 (1993).

Rosemary Haughton, *The Passionate God* (London: Darton, Longman & Todd, 1981).

L. Hay-Cooper, *Josephine Butler and Her Work for Social Purity* (London: SPCK, 1922).

Kathleen Hendry, *Don't Ask Me Why: Sixty Years a Woman Minister* (London: United Reformed Church, 1991).

Florence Hill, *Mission Unlimited: The Story of The Mothers' Union* (London: The Mothers' Union, n.d.).

[Lady] Hosie, *Jesus and Woman* (London: Hodder & Stoughton, 1946).

Josephine Kamm, *How Different from Us* (London: Bodley Head, 1958).

Clifford W. Kew (ed.), *Catherine Booth: Her Continuing Relevance* (London: The Salvation Army, 1990).

Mary Levison, *Wrestling With the Church* (London: Arthur James, 1992).

Florence Li Tim Oi, *Most Beloved Daughter* (London: Darton, Longman & Todd, 1985).

H. S. Marshall, *Pastoralia for Women* (London: SPCK, 1934).

J. R. Miller, *Home-Making or The Ideal Family Life* (London: The Sunday School Union, n.d.).

Ministry of Women, Committee appointed by His Grace the Lord Archbishop of Canterbury (London: SPCK, 1919).

M. Emmanuel Orchard IBVM, *Till God Will* (Darton, Longman & Todd, 1985).

Jeanne Pieper, *The Catholic Woman* (Los Angeles: Lowell House, 1993).

Charles E. Raven, *Women and Holy Orders* (London: Hodder & Stoughton, 1928).

Eleanor S. Riemaer and John C. Fout (eds), *European Women: A Documentary History 1789–1945* (Brighton: The Harvester Press, 1983).

A. Maude Royden, *The Making of Women* (London: George Allen & Unwin Ltd, 1917).

A. Maude Royden, *Political Christianity* (London: G. P. Putman's Sons, 1922).

A. Maude Royden, *Women at the World's Crossroads* (New York: The Women's Press, 1922).

Jane Sheldon (ed.), *Women Talking!* (London: James Clarke & Co. Ltd, 1945).

Ray Strachey, *The Cause* (London: Virago, 1978).

T. S. Taylor, *For Parsons Only* (London: Allenson & Co. Ltd, n.d.)

T. F. Torrance, *The Ministry of Women* (Edinburgh: The Handsel Press, 1992).

Evelyn Underhill, *Worship* (London: Nisbet & Co. Ltd, 1948).

Martha Vicinus, *Independent Women* (London: Virago, 1985).

Westminster Hymnal (London: Burns, Oates & Washbourne, 1953).

Frances E. Willard, *Woman in the Pulpit* (Boston: D. Lothrop Company, 1888).

W. J. Wintle and Florence Witts, *Florence Nightingale and Frances E. Willard* (London: The Sunday School Union, n.d.).